BEING AND NOT-BEING

BEING AND NOT-BEING

AN INTRODUCTION TO
PLATO'S *SOPHIST*

by

PAUL SELIGMAN

MARTINUS NIJHOFF / THE HAGUE / 1974

PRINTED IN THE NETHERLANDS

Contents

Preface

The present monograph on Plato's *Sophist* developed from series of lectures given over a number of years to honours and graduate philosophy classes in the University of Waterloo. It is hoped that it will prove a useful guide to anyone trying to come to grips with, and gain a perspective of Plato's mature thought. At the same time my study is addressed to the specialist, and I have considered at the appropriate places a good deal of the scholarly literature that has appeared during the last thirty years. In this connection I regret that some of the publications which came to my notice after my work was substantially completed (such as Kamlah's and Sayre's) have not been referred to in my discussion.

As few philosophy students nowadays are familiar with Greek I have (except in a few footnotes) translated as well as transliterated all Greek terms. Citations from Plato's text follow Cornford's admirable translation as closely as possible, though the reader will find some significant deviations. The most notable of these concerns the key word *on* which I have rendered throughout as "being," thus avoiding Cornford's "existence" and "reality" which tend to prejudge the issues which the dialogue raises.

I wish to express my gratitude to Father Joseph Owens of the Pontifical Institute in Toronto and to my colleague Prof. D. D. Roberts who have both read my manuscript at an earlier stage and offered most helpful criticisms and suggestions, many of which I have adopted. Naturally the responsibility for the present version remains entirely my own. I am also indebted to many of my former students, in particular to Prof. M. Husain for our stimulating discussions which have greatly furthered my work. Lastly I wish to record my thanks to the University of Waterloo for granting me a term's sabbatical leave which enabled me to put my thoughts in their present form.

Waterloo, Ontario   PAUL SELIGMAN
Fall, 1972

Acknowledgement

The author is grateful to Messrs. Routledge & Kegan Paul Ltd., London and the Humanities Press Inc., New York for permission to quote from F. M. Cornford, *Plato's Theory of Knowledge*.

§ 1. Approach to Plato

In recent discussions of Plato's philosophy more attention has probably been given to the *Sophist* than to any other dialogue. The reason is not far to seek. A large section of contemporary philosophy is concerned with logical and linguistic analysis, and there can be little doubt that the *Sophist* raises problems in these areas which are of considerable relevance even to-day. As a consequence, it is the logical and linguistic aspects of the dialogue that have stolen the limelight. It also seems that Plato invites such approaches, being ostensibly concerned with discourse, i.e., with expressions and statements, and with propositional beliefs. All the same, whatever perplexities he unearths in the *logoi* of Parmenides and his Sophistic stepchildren, he meets them at the ontological level. We may say, then, that in the *Sophist* too, Plato remains ontologically committed.

Some of the most able modern writers on the subject have been aware of this. Thus Mr. Runciman (1962) says that "what we should explain as the logical structure of language is to Plato the ontological structure of reality ..." (p. 121, cp. p. 62), an insight which has not perhaps found sufficient consideration in the body of his book. From a logical point of view, the *Sophist* is prolegomenal. While distinctions between attribution and identity, between various senses of the word "to be" can be ferreted out of Plato's arguments, they do not seem to have been present to his mind in those terms. Where we should speak of negative identity, his locution will be "participation in the other," i.e., he expresses himself in the ontological medium. It seems advisable to approach Plato's thought by considering the expressions he uses as intended by him. They are not "metaphors" (Ryle, 1965, p. 65) that cloud a logical structure, but have a function peculiar to them. Thus we should not, for instance, try to account for his "mingling" and "sharing," which help him to unravel besetting philosophical problems, in terms of our copular "is".

Similarly, his "Forms" and "Kinds" (*eide* and *gene*) are not concepts ("*Begriffe*") in our sense, not even at least concepts (*pace* Ackrill, 1957, p. 207 n. 2). Plato does not, and cannot handle them at our level of conceptual abstraction. As Stenzel reminded us, at *Parm.* 132B f. Plato refutes twice the view that the *eidos* can be comprehended as concept: "the *eide* remain *onta* (things that are), they are not *noēmata* (thoughts) in the soul" (1962, p. 30, Engl. ed. p. 57). They are *objects* of thought. It is true that the *eide* and *gene* of the *Sophist* have shed the paradigm character that attached to forms in the *Phaedo* and the *Republic*. But this does not mean that they are now adequately accounted for as "significations of expressions" (Frede, 1967, p. 94). There is no evidence right down to the *Philebus* that they have ceased to possess being in the fullest sense of the word, i.e., they remain "really real" (*ontos onta*). It is certainly legitimate for us to step outside Plato's philosophy (as he himself was not able to do), to take a meta-view, as it were, and speak of Plato's conception of "form," provided we are not oblivious of its intuitional origin and associations. On those terms, the *eide* and *gene* of the *Sophist* may be regarded as a re-formed "eidos conception". But they do not enter the dialogue as concepts. They enter it as ontological designates. Consequently, the statements which Plato formulates about his "very great kinds" may be classed as what we have come to term "synthetic a priori propositions," rather than as statements of compatibility and negative identity. The relations between the "very great kinds" of the *Sophist* are necessary relations, eternally inscribed in the nature of things. They determine the structure of reality – and hence of our *logoi* about reality – which the student of the Academy was called upon to make articulate in practising the science of dialectic.

The present study has been undertaken with the ontological perspective in mind. In addition the historical roots of Plato's thinking will be emphasized. His struggle with the Eleatic legacy permeates this dialogue in a deeper sense and to a greater degree than has generally been admitted. On the other hand, the value of logically and linguistically oriented exegeses of the *Sophist*, such as have appeared during the last thirty years, is readily acknowledged. Still, they have not given us the whole story; they have neglected a significant dimension of Plato's thinking, and therefore need supplementing, and it only speaks for the richness of his work that it can be approached in more than one way.

My discussion will concentrate on the middle sections of the dialogue and follow the order of its argument, which develops organically and with greater cohesion than its dramatic form and artistic presentation might suggest. There can be no doubt about the seriousness of Plato's concern (contra Peck, 1952, cp. Runciman, 1962, p. 59), but there is also present a tinge of poetic playfulness which can have a baffling effect on readers seeking straightforward, unequivocal answers. At times it looks as though Plato lived up to the Heraclitean word that nature likes to conceal itself. It seems though that on some issues raised in the *Sophist* Plato himself was wavering, that there are others on which he had not made up his mind. In any case, he was never prone to produce a closed and final system, and each dialogue right to the end of his life meant a fresh start. But certain positions he never surrendered, and some of these permeate the *Sophist* as well. One of them is his belief in a rational and intrinsically knowable order of reality. That order is apprehended by the intuitive intellect and capable of being set out, indeed needing to be set out, in reasoned discourse; i.e., it is apprehended by *noësis*, accompanied by *logoi*. As Plato matured, the emphasis shifted from the former to the latter mode. And while the latter takes the stage in the *Sophist*, there is no evidence that the former was abandoned by him even then.

Finally, we may here take note of a persistent tendency in Plato to arrive at more primitive ontological notions,[1] and at the same time to push his initial analysis further back. This tendency had only come to a temporary halt with the "Form of the Good" in the *Republic*. In the *Sophist* the very great kinds, and particularly "Being" and "Not-Being" appear as ultimate determinants. After having made a Socratic ideal the pivot and goal of all that is, Plato's thought moved to purely formal notions which, as we shall see, are devoid of descriptive content. And the fourfold classification in the *Philebus* (23C–26D) can be similarly assessed. What we are witnessing in the *Sophist* thus appears as a significant phase in Plato's progress towards a formalised ontology. We are here considering the very great kinds not as functions in propositions (Moravcsic, 1962) but in regard to their ontological function. They can play the former role, too, but only in virtue of the latter, as I intend to show. The development, in which they stand out, probably culminated in the doctrine of idea-numbers and its two ultimate principles of the "one" and the "indeterminate dyad" (Aristotle, *Metaphys*. A, VI).

---

[1] I speak of "notions" in the context of the development of Plato's thought, similarly as I spoke earlier of his "form conception". I avoid "idea" because of its technical associations. These "notions" name real entities in Plato's ontological schemes, they are Aristotelian *archai* in so far as they are principles both of being and of knowing.

Pari passu with Plato's search for more primitive notions, another movement takes place: from the participation of sensible things in intelligible forms, he directs his attention to participation of forms in forms, thence to participation in forms of an obviously higher order, "forms of forms," as I will call them. The kind of analysis initially applied to sensible things thus comes to be applied to the forms themselves. In this line of development, too, the *Sophist* holds a prominent place.

§ 2. Parmenides, Plato and the Sophists

The "reverend and awful" figure of Parmenides (*Theaet.* 183 E6) looms large over Plato's final encounter with the Sophists. Parmenides' influence on Greek philosophy was profound. The core of his doctrine can be summarised in three statements which we take from his *Way of Truth*; I will call them the Eleatic canon:

The decision rests in this: It is or it is not (fr. VIII, 15 f.). It is, and it is impossible for it not to be (fr. II). It is impossible that things that are-not are (paraphrased from fr. VI and VII).

These impossibilities are logical impossibilities, and Parmenides' words appear as an incipient formulation of the Law of Excluded Middle, for no intermediate position between being and not-being is tolerated. Further, this "law" has here come to birth as the law of being *qua se*, i.e., being absolutely unqualified, and we cannot generalise from it. Any application to specific states of affairs (*Sachverhalte*) is ruled out; only being (*qua se*) is, and there can be nothing besides it (fr. VIII, 37).

(i) Coming to be, passing away, motion and change of quality are impossible since at one point or another they involve what is not. They are the deluded beliefs of mortals, and any mention of them will be mere names, i.e., names that name nothing, senseless babble as we might say (fr. VIII, *passim*).[1]

(ii) What is not can neither be known nor be uttered (fr. II), with the corollary that what can be thought and be said must be (cp. fr. VI). In other words, to think and the thought that it is are the same (fr. III, VIII, 34).

From this we may conclude that intelligible being is the only legiti-

---

[1] On "mere names" (or "empty names") see Taran (1965) 129ff., Guthrie (1965) 41.

mate content of thought and speech. Moreover, it is the "direct object" of thought and speech, not what is thought or spoken *about*.[2] Hence Parmenides' position is epitomized by the phrase: to think and to speak sense is to think and to speak being (cp. fr. VI). The relevance of this formula to the problems raised in the *Sophist* will become apparent.

Succeeding generations of philosophers felt constrained to accept the Eleatic canon but were only able to come to terms with it by circumventing some of its implications. This is true of the cosmologists who, in order to save appearances, posited a plurality of natural entities to each of which they ascribed the logical properties of Parmenides' one being, and were thus enabled to allow for the reality of motion and change. Being, under their hands, was to become matter. Parmenides himself had concerned himself with the deceptive appearances of the sensible world, but for him that was altogether divorced from being and truth. He put his account of it in a separate part of his poem, *The Way of Seeming*, whose content – the opinions of mortals – on his own showing stands condemned as mere names, "a deceptive order of words" (fr. VIII, 52).

Plato, too, was under the spell of his Eleatic heritage, and Parmenides' influence on him must rank next to that of Socrates. Whether he was aware of it or not, his classical form conception was modelled on Parmenides' notion of one being, it was Parmenidoid in character. Only forms were possessed of true being (an expression to which we shall return), they were self-same, single, everlasting and changeless; they belonged to a realm of their own, separate from the changing world of sensible appearances.

But on three counts the Plato of the middle period had already sinned against Parmenides. (i) His forms (as against fr. VIII, 36 f.) had a nature other than being, were something besides being, e.g. beauty itself, the good itself. In accounting for this feature I shall use the phrase "they have a nature of their own," although this is not strictly correct since they *are* the "natures" which they name. (ii) As there are many natures so there are many such forms, many bearers of being, not one. (iii) Plato, like the cosmologists before him, though perhaps for different reasons,[3] attempted to rescue the sensible world from the

---

[2] I am not making a point of grammar here since the Greek verbs *noein* (to think) and *legein* (to say, speak) take the direct object. And so do their English equivalents. But "to think and say being" is idiomatically strained if not absurd, yet represents aptly, I believe, Parmenides' epistemological cramp.

[3] e.g. The sensible world was after all the place where Socratic morality was to be put in practice, where man was given the opportunity to remake his soul.

limbo where Parmenides had consigned it. In the *Republic* he tells us, that it is so constituted that it both is and is not (V, 477A) – a daring paradox in the light of Parmenides' veto.[4] It hovers halfway between being (the forms) and not-being, as opinion lies midway between knowledge and ignorance. But opinion for Plato can be transformed into knowledge; its objects are not "mere names," they are named after the *forms* (see, e.g., *Phaedo* 102B, Aristotle, *Metaphys.* 987b8). They participate in the forms, participate in being. Participation thus spans the chasm between the two Eleatic ways,[5] and it is not surprising that in the dialogue which bears his name Parmenides is made to fire his most powerful broadside against participation, that is against the relation which Plato had tried to establish between "being" and "seeming." But whatever Plato's earlier departures from Father Parmenides, in order to understand his moves in the *Sophist* it is important to realize that he had not yet revised his essentially Parmenidoid form conception, although such revision had become necessary by advances he had made in other directions.

It must remain an open question whether the Sophists merely exploited the Eleatic canon, as Plato seems to suggest, or were genuinely worried by the puzzles which could be generated from it. They were sceptics. But their scepticism can hardly have been due to those puzzles, rather it appears that these underscored, and perhaps were even used to justify an already prevailing attitude. On the other hand, it seems plausible that in a deeper sense Parmenides' philosophy was one of the

[4] This attempted union of the most fundamental opposites is reminiscent of Heraclitus, whose philosophy served in other respects too as a model for Plato's conception of the sensible world (e.g. the flux doctrine), just as Parmenides had fathered the intelligible world of forms. Here Plato seems to defy Parmenides' scathing criticism in fr. VI which may well have been directed against Heraclitus. But whether Plato was conscious that his move represented an infringement of Eleatic principles must remain an open question. He may even have thought that his step was legitimate in the eyes of Parmenides since ostensibly confined to sensible appearances, and therefore a "way of seeming." The crux of the matter though is that it pointed beyond the second to the first way (see above).

[5] It is quite true that there are analogies and even similarities between Parmenides' two ways, e.g. the roles assigned to light and night in proem and cosmogony, and likewise to the bonds of Necessity in fr. VIII, 30 and fr. X. No less striking is the account of mind and thought in fr. XVI, for surely we should expect thought, whose sole object is being, to be barred altogether from the way of seeming. Still, the pronouncements in fr. I, 30 f. establish beyond doubt that there cannot be true conviction in the opinions contained in the latter (see Taran, 1965, ch. II). It is Parmenides' intention to keep the sensible area of motion and change completely separate from being and truth. The separation is a logical one: there is but one sense of "It is" which must, and can only refer to being *qua se*. Whatever falls short of being, that is seeming, gets automatically hooked on not-being. There was not for Parmenides, as there was to be for Plato, a *tertium quid*. On the whole question compare Guthrie (1965) I, A (11), in particular p. 75 f.

roots of 5th century scepticism. If only being in his pure, absolute sense is knowable, then there is nothing more to know, nothing to learn. To escape scepticism it seemed necessary to extend the notion of being which he had bequeathed to philosophy, to bring it back into the world, as it were, from its "immutable, solemn aloofness" (*Soph.* 249 A1 f.), and this the cosmologists attempted to do; or else, as we might put it with a surely permissible linguistic twist, to discern determinate "forms" of being as objects of knowledge, and so of learning – the way of Plato.[6]

The Sophists reacted quite differently. They were enlightened pragmatists and not interested in the question of "being" as it had been raised through two hundred years of Greek philosophy, had been raised by Parmenides, and was again to be raised by Plato. Nor do they appear to have been genuine lovers of truth for its own sake. They were not committed to safeguard being and knowledge. With great sophistication they pushed the scepticism which was seminal in the Eleatic position (though far removed from Parmenides' mind) to its logical extreme, thus effectively reducing his doctrine to absurdity. It seems to have been one of the objects of Plato's *Sophist* to show that their attempts were self-defeating, and that there was a better way of dealing with the Eleatic canon.

In attacking the Parmenidean position, the Sophists appear to have developed two distinct procedures. Firstly they outright inverted it, standing Parmenides on his head as in modern times Marx was said to have stood Hegel on his head. This comes out most notably in a treatise by Gorgias, the rhetorician, in which he attempted to establish contra Parmenides that nothing is, and that if there was anything, it could neither be thought nor be known by men, and even if known not communicated, using arguments of the Eleatic type, some of them identical with those found in the *Way of Truth* (cp. Guthrie, 1969, pp. 192–200). Protagoras' *Homo mensura* doctrine can be seen in a similar light. Against the doctrine of the first way that only being is, it advances the position of the second way: only what seems is. The "opinions of mortals" determine what is and how it is. Seeming is not an aberration from the way of being, but being is a function of seeming (in the mathematical sense of function). As Plato reports it (*Theaet.* 152A, see Kahn, 1966, p. 250), "as each thing seems to me, such it is for me, and as it seems to you, such it is for you – you and I being men."

---

[6] In his account of the Battle of Gods and Giants (*Soph.* 245E ff.) Plato shows great insight into the historical position of his own philosophy.

Infallibility thus attaches no longer to timeless intelligible being as revealed to, and judged by reason, no longer to what is common, or universal as we might prefer to say. Infallibility attaches to the private experiential data of each individual as they happen to occur (cp. *Theaet.* 152C), i.e., in modern parlance, to sensations of the present moment – surely, a complete reversal of Parmenidean *noësis*!

It is the second Sophistic procedure that brings us direct to our dialogue. The Sophists, like everyone else, extended the scope of the Eleatic doctrine, fastening though on not-being rather than being. By a change of direction, which may strike us as modern, they applied it to language, to *logoi*, discourse in general. This is not, however, so surprising a move if we remember that they were teachers of rhetoric and that *logoi* were their stock-in-trade. It is in this area, then, that they generated their puzzles.

Parmenides had said, what is not can neither be thought nor be uttered. The Sophist would argue:

> To say what is false is to say what is not;
> But it is impossible to say what is not;
> Therefore there can be no falsity, and all
>   statements (*logoi*) are true (cp. *Soph.* 260C).

The impossibility of saying what is false had been discussed in the earlier *Euthydemus* (283E–284C; cp. *Cratyl.* 429D f.) and paired there with the view that it is impossible to contradict another person (285D–286C). This in fact is implied by Protagoras' doctrine that what seems to me *is* for me and what seems to you *is* for you, for according to this doctrine, my truth is private to me and your truth is private to you, and there can be no clash. As in the case of Parmenides' own philosophy the impossibilities here invoked have logical force.

Following Socrates, Plato had struggled with the Sophists throughout his philosophical career. The present dialogue is explicitly directed to them, a final reckoning, as it were. The Sophist is to be unmasked as what he *is*, his talk to be shown up for what it is worth – deceptive falsehoods. We can see Plato's difficulty. The quintessence of the Sophist's falsehoods is his denial, on the authority of Parmenides, that falsity is possible, from which it follows that his "falsehoods" are necessarily true. Therefore his crucial assertion that falsity is impossible can itself not be false either. It cannot be disproved. Put differently, to deny what the Sophist affirms is to affirm what is not. But this is impossible. Hence he cannot be contradicted. And for the same

9

reason the affirmation that it is impossible to contradict him can itself not be contradicted. Either way, the Sophist wins.

Plato shows himself aware of the difficulty. In his poetic way he puts it thus:

The Sophist takes refuge in the darkness of not-being: where he is at home and has the knack of feeling his way; and it is the darkness that makes him so hard to perceive (*Soph.* 254A 4–6).[7]

The Sophist, then, is "the sort of creature that is hard to hunt down," and his lair will not yield to frontal assault. To dislodge him Plato must go back to the source of his aberration and join issue with Parmenides himself; he must show that it *is* possible, and in which sense it is possible, to think and say what is not, and so what is false.

Thus Plato's debate with the Sophist is to bring him face to face with the Eleatic canon which had determined much of his thinking, though perhaps no more than half-consciously. While, as we have noticed, he had infringed it in certain respects, there had been no open confrontation, no explicit defiance, for too much of it had been built into his theory of ideas. Now, however, as though awakened from a dogmatic slumber, he will face up to it in all its implications and raise the proscribed question: what is that feared "not-being"? As a result the lethal Parmenidean sting will be taken out of the "is-not" and the Eleatic dichotomy – "It is or it is not" – dismantled. This in turn involves the question, what is being?, bringing in its train a revision of the classical form conception insofar as it had been modelled on the Parmenidean notion of being. It will shed its Parmenidoid character.

This links up with the stage of Plato's progress at the time of writing the *Sophist*, e.g.

(a) with his own previous criticisms of the theory of forms in the *Parmenides*;

(b) with the development of the science of dialectic, put forward in quite general terms in the *Republic*, but subsequently spelled out in detail in the *Phaedrus*, which made the isolation of forms from one another, as self-contained Parmenidoid ones, obsolete;

(c) with the inconclusiveness of the discussion of falsity in the *Theaetetus*.

---

[7] He is presently contrasted with "the philosopher, whose thoughts constantly dwell upon the nature of being, and who is difficult to see because the region is so bright; for the eye of the vulgar soul cannot endure to keep its gaze fixed on the divine" (254 A8–B1). Taking these two passages together, we may notice a cryptic allusion to Parmenides' journey from night to light where truth and being are revealed to him by a goddess (fr. I). The same motif seems to underlie the ascent of the prisoner from the cave in the *Republic*.

The dramatic date of the *Sophist* is the day following the *Theaetetus*, and Theaetetus himself is again the respondent. But in contrast to the earlier dialogue Socrates is no longer the interrogator. This is consistent with Plato's changed attitude to Parmenides as well as to the theory of ideas which up to then had been propounded through the mouth of Socrates. This was understandable enough insofar as it had been devised as an ontological basis for Socrates' quest for definitions, and in the middle dialogues the forms had fitted the bill for Socratic moral ideals. The theory now ceases to be an "ideal theory," and the once predominant interest in moral forms recedes (cp. Stenzel, 1961, p. 1 f., Engl. ed. p. 23 f.).

Socrates' place is taken by a Stranger from Elea, Parmenides' home town. So we might expect a staunch Parmenidean, or at least a Zeno (as in the *Parmenides*) who places his eristic gifts at the master's service. Far from it! The Stranger is introduced as a serious and distinguished philosopher, but his business is – parricide. The choice of this figure seems to reflect an acknowledgement on the part of Plato of his indebtedness to Eleatic thinking; and although he must now break away from it, it is still through an Elean that he will speak. It also fits in well with Plato's native reticence that he lets an Elean attack the Eleatic citadel, and at the same time express his (i.e. Plato's own) scruples about such daring venture (e.g. 242 A f., § 6 below).[8]

---

[8] For quite a different reason for the choice of the Stranger, see Gilbert Ryle (1966) p. 27 f.

§ 3. The seventh Division and the Statement of the Problem: 233D–237B

In order to unmask the Sophist we need to understand his art. To understand his art we must define it, and to define it we need to employ the method of division. Right from the start the scene is set against the background of the new science of dialectic.

The first six attempts end in failure. This is not surprising since we are told repeatedly that the Sophist is an evasive creature which is hard to catch, and these six abortive divisions cannot be dismissed as an exercise in irrelevant mockery. Plato's educational concern is never absent from his literary work. The student of the Academy required training in dialectic, and this must have involved a good deal of trial and error. Like many Platonic dialogues the *Sophist* has its didactic aspect. As it grapples with what may well have been the most tantalizing *aporia* (perplexity) in the history of Greek thought, it displays magisterially the philosopher's practice.

The seventh division, which will eventually be successful, brings us to the core problem. Image making (*mimetike, eidolopoiike*) is the art to which the practice of the Sophist will be seen to belong. But in order to track him down, image making must be methodically divided. This gives us two kinds: the making of likenesses (*eikastike*) and the making of semblances (*phantastike*). The distinction, though subsequently blurred, regains importance towards the end of the dialogue. Likenesses (*eikones*) are exact copies, faithfully reproducing the proportions of their models. Semblances (*phantasmata*)[1] are created by artists, who

---

[1] I have adopted Cornford's rendering of *phantasmata* as "semblances," although this to some extent prejudges the issue, and "appearances" (Fowler) is possible, in particular as later in the dialogue the cognate *phantasia* (e.g. 264A) requires to be rendered as "appearance." On the other hand, the Sophist's verbal *phantasmata* are introduced in explicit contradistinction from likenesses (*eikones*), and further characterised as "appearing without really being" and as "deceptive." Therefore "semblances" seems to correspond to Plato's intentions.

are not interested in truth and put in their images proportions that seem to be beautiful but are not like the original.[2] Similarly the Sophist creates semblances in discourse, spoken images that seem to be true but cannot stand up to the facts encountered in actual life (234D–E). What the Sophist produces in his discourse appears to be (*phainesthai*), seems to be (*dokein*) but is really not (*me einai*). It is not, yet it deceives. The semblance of truth without *being* true must be something, otherwise the Sophist could not ply his trade. His falsehoods must be meaningful and this for Plato entails real being (*ontos einai*). Yet a falsehood asserts what is not. Hence we are involved in the contradiction that what is-not has being. The position is summarised at 236E:

This appearing or seeming but not being, and saying something which yet is not true – all these [expressions] have always been and still are deeply involved in perplexity. It is extremely difficult to find correct terms in which one may say or think that falsehoods really are without being caught in a contradiction in uttering such words.

In this quotation "saying something" signifies "saying what is" (saying something that has reference), as well as speaking sense or speaking meaningfully. Conversely "saying nothing" signifies "saying what is-not" (saying something that does not refer to anything), as well as speaking without sense or meaning.[3] Therefore the gist of the phrase is, "how can we speak meaningfully when we say what is not true = what is false = what is-not?" Truth is here assimilated to both being and meaning, and falsity to not-being as well as lack of meaning.[4] For Plato, as for his predecessors any expression to be meaningful must refer to something that is; a name must name something or somebody; otherwise it will be a "mere name" or as Plato will later put it, it will be but the name of a name (244 D8).[5] Hence the problem: in which

---

[2] There is an analogy here, but no more than an analogy, with the artisan's bed which is like the form of the bed, and the artist's distorted version of the artisan's creation, in *Republ.* X. In the *Sophist* the models of both image- and semblance-maker are actually existing things, and the forms do not come into the present passage.

[3] Compare Cornford (1935), p. 205, Ackrill (1955), p. 203, Moravcsic (1962), p. 26.

[4] This dichotomy will eventually be broken down: both true and false statements are meaningful, and both involve being as well as not-being.

[5] Parmenides thought that the "deceitful order of words" in his second way enunciated "mere names"; if so, Plato would hold that it could not have been deceitful. On the other hand, there are perhaps sufficient similarities between the two ways to lend the second way a "semblance" of truth; see p. 7 n. 5 and Guthrie (1965) *loc. cit.* While the Eleatic canon disallowed any connection between the two realms, we find Plato in our dialogue endeavouring to assign an ontological foundation to Sophistic *phantasmata*, similarly as he assigned it to sensible appearances in the *Republic*.

sense can falsehoods refer?[6] How can what is-not have being? It is the central question of the dialogue.

In the *Sophist*, as already remarked, Plato is ostensibly concerned with expressions, with discourse; "appearing" and "seeming" are coupled with deceptive *logoi*. Ontology enters through the identification of "what is false" with "what is-not" and the ensuing necessity to ascribe being to what is-not. But the metaphysical status of sensible appearances which are copies of forms, which occupied Plato in the middle dialogues, is here not his concern. It is spoken images that are in question. In fact, the usual similes, such as reflections in mirrors or water, or even artefacts (which were brought in earlier in the dialogue, p. 12 f. above) will explicitly be excluded from the debate with the Sophist, who

will profess to know nothing about mirrors or water or even eyesight, and will confine his question to what can be gathered from discourse (239 E7 ff.).

Yet, it will take Plato a long road to reach the being of false *logoi*. In the first place he will investigate and clear out of the way the Eleatic notion of absolute not-being [the contradictory of absolute being] (§ 4). Next he will raise the question of the being of images (§ 5); this will lead him to a (provisional) definition of false *logos*, and the crucial challenge of the Eleatic canon (§ 6). This in turn will involve the question "what is being?", and there follow critical discussions of accounts of "being" by previous philosophers, including Parmenides and Plato's own classical theory of ideas (§§ 7–11). Thus we are carried to the central doctrines of the dialogue: the communion of forms, the ontology of the "very great kinds," and the definitive dismantling of the "is – is not" dichotomy, which is to provide new significance for all "is-not" statements (§§ 12–20). Finally we are given an account of the nature of *logoi*, and of the being of false *logoi* (§§ 21–24). The seventh division can then be completed; and the dialogue ends with a definition of the art of Sophistry.

[6] It is important to note that at this stage of the argument there is as yet no clear distinction between names that do not name and falsehoods that do not refer, that is, no clear distinction between the function of statements and the function of names or words. This distinction will not be made until very much later in the dialogue.

§ 4. Absolute Not-being: 237B–239C

Plato singles out the absolute Parmenidean sense of not-being as "that which is in no way whatever" (*to medamos on*) so as to leave himself leeway for offering eventually his own non-Parmenidean interpretation of not-being. The Stranger begins by noting that we do not hesitate to utter the expression, but to what can it be applied? Surely not to anything that is, and therefore not to "something." For we use the word "something" of something that is, not in "naked isolation" from the things that are [i.e. as a non-denoting abstraction]. Therefore the expression "that which is in no way whatever" is non-referring. Then, playing on the ambiguities of "saying something" and of "saying nothing," already mentioned, the Stranger notes that a person uttering the expression is not saying anything, i.e., since he cannot refer to anything, he does not speak sense – he says nothing.

But the expression is not only non-referring, it is also non-descriptive. To what-is we attribute something else that is. But surely, we cannot attach what-is to what is-not. We are even prevented from giving it the minimal determination of number (which for Plato *is* in the most thoroughgoing sense). We cannot say that it is one or that it is many. Obviously we must speak neither of what is-not (in the singular) nor of things that are-not (in the plural). But it is equally impossible to think or speak of not-being *qua se* (*to me on auto kath' hauto*), i.e. without any determination (238 C8–10, cp. 239 B7–10). Nay, even this very statement affirming the inexpressibility of not-being is inadmissible, for it was itself couched in the singular, using the definite article *to*. The Stranger concludes that since we can ascribe neither being nor unity or plurality to absolute not-being, we must remain silent about it.

It is obvious (though the point is not made) that Parmenides himself should not have mentioned it; but he had to mention it because his notion of being was contrast dependent. While he dismissed it, not unlike Plato now, from his "Way of Truth," he had to put it in a separate part of his poem and cash it as "seeming." Plato does not accept the equation "seeming" = absolute not-being = nothing. Absolute not-being will not help us to solve the riddle of "appearing or seeming but not being" (236 E, p. 13 above), will not help us to account for falsehood, for the Sophist's semblances.

In contradistinction to Parmenides', Plato's dismissal of *to medamos on* (the Eleatic *to me on*) is total, and whatever notion of being he will entertain in the *Sophist*, it will not be contrast dependent. For the earlier Plato, too, being had been contrast dependent, not indeed on not-being, but on becoming; further *qua* intelligible on the sensible, and *qua* changeless on the changeable. In the *Sophist* Plato will wrestle, not only with the Parmenidean dichotomy, but with his own polarities as well.

§ 5. The Being of Images: 239C–240C

The upshot of the preceding section is that the inability to find terms in which to define Parmenidean not-being has made the Sophist's position "impenetrable." He can now turn the tables against us when we accuse him of creating semblances in his *logoi*, for of these we have said that "they seem to be but are really not" (p. 13 above).[1] The next move must therefore be to show that semblances are, i.e., possess being, and in which sense they possess being.

Image (*eidolon*) is the generic term which covers both likeness (*eikon*) and semblance (*phantasma*) as distinguished earlier. In a decisive passage (240 A–B) the Stranger sets out to determine the ontological status, the being of *eidolon* but ends up with the being of *eikon*. The context, however, with its immediately preceding reference to the Sophist's art of semblance making (239 C9 f.) favours the conclusion that his wares are covered as well. The passage may be quoted in full:

(240 A7) Theaetetus: Well, Stranger, what can we say an image is except another thing of the same sort copied from the true one?
Stranger: Do you mean another true one, or in what sense do you speak of it as "of the same sort"?
Th.: In no wise a true one but one seeming like it (*eoikos*).
Str.: Meaning by true a thing that really is?
Th.: Quite so.
Str.: And by not true the opposite of the true one?
Th.: Of course.
Str.: Then by "what seems like" you mean what has not real being, if you say it is not true.
Th.: But it is in a way.
Str.: Only not truly, according to you.
Th.: No, except that it is really a likeness (*eikon*).
Str.: So not having real being, it really *is* what we call a likeness.[2]

---

[1] This must surely be the sense of 239 C f., contra Cornford (1935) p. 210, n. 1: the Sophist *does* lurk in the region of Parmenidean not-being; cp. 254 A 4–6, quoted p. 10 above.

[2] Or on an alternative rendering: Then what we call a likeness, though not really being, really *is*.

17

The result is that the *eidolon* has real being *qua eidolon*. It has not real being in the sense of being true. The original is true, the image only "seems like" the original. We noticed earlier an assimilation of truth to being (236 E and comments p. 13 f.) such as was most strikingly evinced in Parmenides where the way of truth had to be the way of being, and the way of being was the true way. Cornford (1935) in the quoted passage rendered "true" (*alethinos*) as "real", and Runciman (1962, p. 68) points out that Plato does not draw any clear distinction between existent, real and true (*on, ontos,* and *alethinos*).[3] Kahn (1966) comments on the rich content of the Greek verb "to be" which *inter alia* connotes truth and genuineness. It seems, however, that in the passage we are here considering the symbiosis between truth and being is beginning to break up, which in itself is a significant step towards conceptual differentiation. Moreover, this step forces itself upon Plato because he wishes to ascribe real being to images, while obliged to reserve truth and genuineness to their originals.

Readers may be reminded that the images with which we are here concerned are spoken images (cp. 240 A 1 f.). Similarly, that there is no indication that the true things which the images copy are forms; they are things that are (*onta*), and thus they may refer to things in general, to states of affairs, or facts in brief. This deserves special mention in so far as the application of "real being" had formerly been restricted to the forms. Now, however, it does not only attach to things in general but even to their images, though to the latter, we must add, *qua* images, and only *qua* images. This may be taken as an indication that although Plato's universe has become more variegated, basic ontological distinctions have not altogether been thrown overboard. This is also suggested by the concluding sentences of our passage where it is pointed out that there seems to be an interweaving of not-being with being. But this is still looked upon as a perplexity (*aporia*), and the blame is squarely put on the Sophist's shoulders who, against our will, has coerced us to admit that not-being in a sense *is*. For a moment it looks as though Plato shies away from an outright confrontation with Parmenides; he will, however, challenge him presently (§ 6).

The not-being which has here got entangled with being is of course no longer the unmentionable absolute not-being which has just been

---

[3] For reasons which will gradually emerge I avoid such renderings as "existent," "exists" etc., using instead "what is," "being," "is," as the context may require. I have to render *ontos*, which literally means "beingly," as "really" because this is a requirement of the English idiom. I shall sometimes use "reality" in speaking about Plato's philosophy, but not as a term designated *in* Plato's philosophy.

eliminated from the dialogue (§ 4). The term "interweaving" (or "weaving together"), *symploke* (240 C1) only occurs twice more in the dialogue (§ 21 f. below) where it will play a crucial role; it should therefore not pass unnoticed.

A word needs to be added to differentiate the union of being and not-being which is here in question from the one which Plato invoked for sensibles in the *Republic* (p. 7 above). Images as spoken of in the *Sophist* are not like sensible things, constituted by an unknowable flux (assimilated to not-being) and forms (being) in which they participate. They possess being *qua* what they are (viz. images) and not-being *qua* what they are not (viz. the originals of which they are copies). But there is also a significant similarity. Both the objects of opinion in the *Republic* and the spoken images in the *Sophist* represent a *tertium quid* between the two horns of the Parmenidean dilemma. But while the former occupy a midway position on a scale between being and not-being, there is no such scale on which we might place the latter. There are no degrees of reality in the *Sophist*. There are forms, things, states of affairs, and there are also images, each of them having real being as what they are.

§ 6. False Logos and the Challenge to Parmenides: 240C–242B

Much of what is contained in this section has been anticipated in § 2 and § 3. The Stranger returns to his over-all goal to define sophistry as the art of semblance making, the art of deception. But although it has been suggested that this involves a *symploke* of not-being with being, we are as yet nowhere near to establishing even the possibility of this position.

We are still under the spell of Parmenides: if anyone is deceived by the Sophist he will be thinking or believing (*doxazein*) things contrary to the things that are, viz. things that are not. Drawing on earlier argument (§ 4) we can say that this does not mean believing that things which are in no way whatever (*ta medamos onta*), somehow are, for these are unthinkable. But it will still mean believing (i) that things which are-not [and the "are-not" is as yet unexplored] are in some way, and (ii) that things which certainly are, are in no way whatever (*medamos einai*).[1]

The Stranger next gives a corresponding account of false statements. This seems justified on the strength of his description of thought as a voiceless dialogue of the soul with itself (263 E). At *Theaet.* 189E f., a similar view had been tentatively put forward. For Plato, dialogue, the Socratic art of question and answer was the paradigm of philosophical reasoning, whether in thought or speech. This does not, however, imply that for him all thinking was discursive, for as he points out (*ibid.*), such silent dialogue will end in a decision which will either come slowly or "in a sudden rush," and this suggests "intuitively" – "like a blaze kindled by a leaping spark" (*Epistol.* VII, 341D, cp. 344B).

---

[1] In mentioning the unmentionable Plato is inconsistent, for (ii) cannot but offend against the veto in § 4. But perhaps this can here pass as a metaphor since it refers to thinking which results from Sophistic deception: the Sophist is an illusionist who can make facts evaporate into "absolute nothingness" as it were. (Or am I too charitable towards Plato?)

A false statement, then, states either (a) that things which are, are-not, or (b) that things which are-not, are.[2] At this point the Stranger from Elea seems forced to side with the Sophist, for earlier on (238 A7 p. 15) he had insisted himself that we must not attach being to what is-not. The context is different though, for "what is-not" in the earlier section did duty for *to medamos on*, absolute not-being, since declared unmentionable. Nevertheless the Sophist would still be justified in pointing to the inconsistency in view of the Stranger's own Parmenidoid, and therefore near Sophistic, definition of false *logos*. The Stranger of course will not be able to give a new sense to this definition, until he has re-interpreted not-being, and he cannot do that until he has dismantled the Parmenidean dichotomy. Therefore he must challenge Parmenides, and this he is now going to do, though still hesitantly and almost apologetically. It is first and foremost against Parmenides, and only derivatively against the Sophist that the position must be established

that what is-not, in some respect *is*, and that, on the other hand, what is, in a way is-not (241 D 5–7).

Only then will it be permissible to talk of false statement and false thinking (or belief) in terms of images or likenesses or copies or semblances without being forced into self-contradiction (241 E).

---

[2] The two modes of false statement (a) and (b) appear in the reverse order of the modes of false thinking (i) and (ii); nothing turns on this. Plato will eventually come up with a definition of false *affirmations* [(b) and (i)]. As he is concerned with not-being, he will also give a great deal of attention to is-not statements in general, but he will not offer an account of false *denials* [(a) and (ii)], and in fact on the interpretation of not-being which he is going to work out, he would not have been able to deal with them satisfactorily (see § 24 below). Here he needs both (b)–(i) and (a)–(ii) in order to formulate his challenge to Parmenides.

§ 7. Being – the Pluralists: 242B–244B

Through the Stranger's mouth Plato confesses that in his younger days he felt no qualms when somebody spoke about not-being. He was sure he understood, but now he is profoundly perplexed by it. May the position not be similar with regard to being?

We profess to be quite at ease about being and to understand the word when it is spoken, though we may not understand not-being – but perhaps we are equally in the dark about both (243 C 3–5).

Plato is aware of the interdependence of the two notions in the Eleatic canon so that a re-interpretation of the one must involve the other as well. Moreover, the uncertainty about being which he here expresses reflects also an uncertainty about his form conception, the Platonic vehicle of being *par excellence*.

He begins with "being," on which everyone seems readily agreed but which for that very reason may harbour secret confusions. And these become soon apparent as we survey the diverging views of earlier philosophers. Among the doctrines alluded to we can discern the early Ionians, the mythologist Hesiod, Heraclitus[1] and Empedocles as well as the Eleatics. All of them undertook to tell us the number (*posa* – how many) and nature (*poia*) of things that are (242 C5–6), but they have treated us like children and talked over our heads – a delightful specimen of Socratic irony from the mouth of an Elean!

Let us then try to find out what those who used the word "being" believed it to signify (243 D3–5).[2] In the present section we address

---

[1] "Parting asunder it is always drawn together" (242 E 2–3) sounds like an actual quotation from Heraclitus; cp. fr. 10.

[2] Being is here chosen from a number of notions which occur in earlier philosophy as "the greatest and most important one" (243 D1). This anticipates its subsequent inclusion among the very great or greatest kinds (*megista gene*). It is noticeable that Plato has no other means to indicate the "meta-character" of being than speaking of it in the superlative. (On meta-character see §§ 11, 13 f. below.)

ourselves to a philosopher who posits more than one thing that is, appropriating being to two or more constituents of the universe, e.g. the hot and the cold. It may be Anaximander whom Plato has here in mind.[3] He puts this question to him:

You who say that hot and cold or some such pair *are* all things, what exactly does this expression convey that you apply to both when you say that they both *are* and each of them *is*? How are we to understand this "to be" you speak of (243 D8–E2)?

There are three alternatives which Plato considers:

(i) Being is a third thing alongside (*para*) hot and cold. If so, there will *be* three things not two.

(ii) We give the name "being" to only one of the two, then the other will not *be* [for hot is not cold], and there will be one thing, not two.

(iii) We may call both together being, but in this case too, there will only be one thing not two, viz. the "hot and cold."

All three alternatives are inconsistent with the hot and cold dualism to which they are offered.

Plato's alternatives seem to rest on three assumptions:

(1) The assumption that any name must refer to something (cp. pp. 13, 14, 15 above); and "being" is treated as a name.

(2) The Eleatic assumption that "being" must refer to one (and not more than one) thing, i.e., either to one alongside the two, or to either the one or the other of the two, or to the two together whereby they are welded into one.

(3) The naturalistic assumption that being must be a specific thing, i.e., either h or c or (h + c) or another thing coordinate with h and c.[4] If Plato had not made assumption (3) on behalf of Anaximander,[5] he might have come to his rescue, as Cornford (1935), p. 220, would wish him to and said, being is neither h nor c nor (h + c) but indeed a third (superlative) thing in which both h and c severally participate. Plato,

---

[3] Anaximander held that the hot and the cold were the primary cosmic opposites separated off from the originating *apeiron* (infinite), and that all things came from them. Although aware of the genealogical mode of archaic thinking (242D), Plato here seems to impute to Anaximander the view that all things which are, are constituted by the hot and the cold, for which I see no justification. Plato is not a historian of philosophy, and quite generally there was no exacting standard of historical veracity in ancient times comparable to our own.

[4] h = hot, c = cold, (h + c) = "hot and cold".

[5] Strictly speaking, Anaximander was not a naturalist in this sense, for his *apeiron*, the originating ruler of all things that *are*, is *ex nomine* indefinite, i.e., nothing specific whatsoever. Plato, however, had no use for the Anaximandrian principle. His thinking on the infinite was determined by Pythagorean doctrines as becomes clear in the *Philebus* and his unwritten doctrine (cp. p. 3 above).

however, was right to make the assumption, and not to obtrude anachronistically his own theory of ideas at this point. In any case, the latter has now gone into the melting pot, for "being" has gone into the melting pot.

Assumption (2) leads us to the next section.

§ 8. Being – the Monists (Parmenides): 244B–245E

Now then we will come to grips with Eleatic being, and it can be readily seen that the skirmish with the h and c philosophers was but an opening gambit. The present discussion is to clear the air for the eventual dissolution of the being/not-being dichotomy. Moreover it has special significance in so far as Plato's criticisms of Parmenidean being will with equal force apply to the Parmenidoid character of his own classical form conception (cp. p. 10 above). The section can conveniently be divided into two parts.

A. Parmenides had deduced from his canon a number of logical properties of being, two of which are singled out by Plato: (i) Being is one, *hen* (fr. VIII, 6), and (ii) being is whole, *oulon* (fr. VIII, 4, 38); to (i) also belongs the property of uniqueness or singleness, *mounogenes* (fr. VIII, 4), to which Plato alludes in the course of his argument.[1]

Plato does not seem to be fair to Parmenides on a number of issues. To begin with, he ought to have said that while the h and c philosophers ascribed being to some [natural] properties, Parmenides ascribed certain [logical] properties to being. Maybe that he feels tied down by his programme to enquire into the views of previous philosophers concerning the *number* of things that are (p. 22 above). Thus he will not say that Parmenides ascribed unity, i.e. the property of being "one," to being, but instead makes it Parmenides' starting point that there is one single (thing), and then adds that he (Parmenides) also gives the name "being" to something (244 B12), i.e., he inverts the logical order of Parmenides' thought.[2]

Since names to be meaningful must refer (see assumption (1), p. 23 above), we are left either with two things, corresponding to the two names "being" and "one," or with two names for one single thing. I

[1] On *mounogenes* see Taran (1965), p. 92.
[2] On Plato's misrepresentation of Parmenides cp. Taran (1965), p. 270.

think the latter alternative would have been acceptable to Parmenides provided we agreed that "one" is not the "first" but the "second" name in the sense that unity is implied by absolute being. But without considering this possibility, Plato makes another move which is not warranted by anything Parmenides said. He suggests that names themselves have being, so that if there is only one thing we cannot give it even one name without finding ourselves landed with two things.[3] If, to escape this, we hold that the name is the same as its *nominatum* it follows either that it names nothing or that it is but the name of a name (244 D8–9). Both alternatives must mean that it is a mere name in Parmenides' sense which implies not-being (cp. pp. 5 and 13 above). It seems obvious that Plato is anxious to maintain that things that are have a nature of their own apart from being, and that those natures are not mere names (cp. p. 6 above), and he has already indicated that this is even the case concerning the Sophist's falsehoods. Here he attempts to vindicate his position in the face of the Eleatic canon by a counter-attack, showing that Parmenides' own pronouncements concerning being fall in the category of mere names, i.e. not-being. In other words, if there is only one thing it is unthinkable and unutterable, and therefore incommunicable. Parmenides is condemned to silence, and the result regarding Parmenidean being turns out no different from that regarding Parmenidean not-being. Moreover, Parmenides has been manoeuvred into a position that is hardly distinguishable from Gorgias' scepticism (p. 8 above), and is even reminiscent of the Heraclitean Cratylus "who finally did not think it right to say anything but only moved his finger" (Arist. *Metaphys.* 1010a 12) – surely a caricature (though perhaps a consequence) of all that Parmenides stood for.

Instead of invoking the being of names, Plato might simply have pointed to an inconsistency on the part of Parmenides. He might have referred to fr. VIII, 36 f. where Parmenides affirms that there is nothing besides being,[4] and have charged him with what he (Plato) had done himself, viz. associating properties other than being itself, with being. In brief, his line of attack might have been that, on the strength of his canon, Parmenides was not entitled to ascribe anything whatever to being.

B. So far, then, Plato has only produced a dubious *ad hominem* argument against the Parmenidean notion. The Stranger next turns to

[3] To raise the question of the being of the name "being" lay beyond Parmenides' conceptual reach.
[4] To be understood in the absolute sense of being *qua se.*

26

holon (= *oulon*), whole,[5] and it is correctly pointed out by Theaetetus that for Parmenides "whole" has the same reference as "being" and "one." Quoting the sphere simile (fr. VIII, 43 ff.) the Stranger insists that "being" thus described must have a centre and extremes, and therefore parts (*mere*).[6] It must be a whole of parts and therefore can not be "one". Still, he concedes that it may be affected by the one in so far as it is a totality or whole of parts, each of which is one, i.e., possesses unity (245 A1–3). But it cannot be unity itself,[7] for unity by definition is without parts. From this the Stranger draws two conclusions: (a) all things must be more than one, which of course is incompatible with Parmenidean monism (245 B8–9), and (b) in virtue of being [merely] affected by unity "being" is not a whole, i.e., as we might put it, it is not a unified whole.[8]

At this point it is important to note that wholeness for Parmenides is not equivalent with a totality of parts. On his view being has no parts, and like the sphere, is whole in the sense of being complete in itself; it is entire and self-sufficient.[9]

The Stranger next makes the point that if being is not a whole and wholeness itself (*auto to holon*) is, then being will fall short of itself,[10] a conclusion which would be in agreement with fr. VIII, 32 where Parmenides points out that it is not right for being to be incomplete. As we just said, to be whole and to be complete are almost interchange-

---

[5] *holon* may be rendered as "whole," or with the article (*to holon*) as "the whole," that which is whole, or "wholeness." The Greek idiom uses adjectives both attributively and in the neuter singular as nouns. Thus we have

to on – that which is, being;

to hen – that which is one, the one, unity;

tauton – the same, that which is the same, sameness;

thateron – the other (the different), that which is other (different), otherness (difference). The last two terms will be met with later on in the text. These multiple usages are a source of ambiguities which cannot always be cleared up.

[6] Not mindful of his own similes, Plato has taken Parmenides' image as referring to an entity instead of comprehending it symbolically. The sphere in Parmenides' thinking is the prototype of homogeneity and uniformity, not an aggregate of constituent parts.

[7] This is the terminology usually reserved for Platonic forms. In using it here the Stranger seems to suggest that while being may be affected by unity (through its parts) the two are distinct kinds and, contra Parmenides, cannot have the same denotation, i.e., cannot be two names of a single thing.

[8] Taking *ekeinou* (245 C2), with Cornford contra Moravcsic (1962, p. 31 n. 3) as referring to *hen*, not to *holon*. I take Plato here to answer the similarly phrased question of 245B 4 f., whether being can be one and whole in virtue of being [merely] affected by unity.

[9] Self-sufficiency remained a Greek ideal, still traceable in Aristotle; see e.g. *Eth.Nic.* X, 7.

[10] Here again wholeness, like unity before, is referred to in terms appropriate to Platonic forms, and the implication would be analogous: Contra Parmenides, wholeness itself and being itself cannot have the same denotation, although (as in the case of unity) being may somehow be affected by wholeness in so far as it is a whole of parts.

able terms for Parmenides.[11] But if being falls short of itself, it will be deprived of being and therefore will not be (245 C5–6). We have come full circle, have we not?

Lastly, if we assume that there is no such thing as wholeness at all, we should be faced with the following consequences (245 C11–D10):

(i) Since what comes to be always comes to be as a whole, no one who does not reckon wholeness among the things that are, must be allowed to speak of being or coming into being.

(ii) What is not a whole cannot have any quantitative determination, for that must apply to a thing as a whole.

Neither (i) nor (ii) are relevant to Parmenides who championed wholeness (in his sense), denied coming into being and was not concerned with a quantitative determination of being.[12]

As against Parmenides' absolute being, the second group of arguments (B) is no more successful than the first (A), and we might be tempted to dismiss the whole section if it did not bear testimony to a significant evolution in Plato's own thinking. As he gradually frees himself from the Eleatic spell, he cannot help being unfair to Parmenides, for it is in contradistinction from, and against the latter's undifferentiated ontological monism that he will develop his own complex position. This comes out in at least two ways:

(i) Parmenides' thinking centred around the simple "it is and cannot not-be," and to say something positive about it, he affirmed its unity and wholeness. We find Plato on the move, as it were, from "it is" to "what is," i.e., to things that have come into being and are. "What is" is not "being *qua se*," although being is one of its determinants, unity another, wholeness a third. These are three distinct factors which are different from, and coordinate with one another. They are second order forms or kinds in so far as they are quite unspecific: yet they are seen to be involved in everything that is.[13] The mutual differentiation of being, unity and wholeness anticipates the doctrine of the *megista gene* which will occupy us later.[14]

---

[11] Cornford (1935, p. 225) although referring to fr. VIII, 32 seems wrong in suggesting that being would be incomplete in the sense that there is "something real," viz. wholeness which it does not include.

[12] Note again Plato's stress on quantitative determination, that is number, as previously in his criticism of absolute not-being (p. 15 above).

[13] "What is" must of course be something specific, i.e., have a nature of its own over and above such formal determination. But this is not suggested in the present section.

[14] In passing it should be noted that neither unity nor wholeness will be included among the very great kinds (see p. 57 below).

(ii) Plato, missing the Parmenidean sense of "wholeness" and the significance of his sphere simile, holds that we can only speak of anything as a whole if it is a whole of parts (cp. *Parm.* 137C). This is of immediate relevance to his *eidos* conception. In the classical theory of ideas the forms were thought of as Eleatic unities. Now, however, forms too must be wholes of parts. This shedding of their Parmenidoid character had become overdue with the development of the science of dialectic. For dialectic proceeds by dividing forms into forms, and the forms into which a generic form is divided are called its parts (*mere*). Thus in the section on dialectic (see p. 53 below) Plato will speak of "wholes" that are traversed and divided (253 C3, D8). The fact that a division is carried out through a whole range of forms, i.e. all forms of a certain generic character, is less significant here than that it is carried through wholes, i.e. through forms which severally are themselves wholes.[15] What then happens to the (Parmenidoid) unity that was formerly affirmed of them? From what has been argued so far concerning being, we are entitled to infer that the forms *qua* vehicles of being, while not the same as unity itself, can be affected by unity in virtue of their unitary parts: and these parts would be the forms into which they can ultimately be divided, i.e., the *infimae species* at which the division of a generic form must come to a halt. Thus both unity and plurality will henceforth be intrinsic to the nature of forms. This seems to be a positive result of Plato's somewhat misplaced criticism of Eleatic being.

[15] Cp. Stenzel (1961) p. 66, Engl. ed. p. 100 f.; also Cornford's comments (1935) p. 269.

§ 9. Being – Materialists and Idealists: 245E–248A

The Stranger has concluded what he wanted to say about philosophers who gave an "exact account" of being, although he has not dealt with all of them. Why exact? We remember that they tried to tell us the number (*posa*) and nature (*poia*) of things that are (p. 22 above). The philosophers considered so far attempted to give precise answers to the first question – the h and c philosophers posited two things, Parmenides one. Those next to be considered would have to answer the first question in terms of an indefinite plurality of things that are, and this would be a sufficient reason for Plato to affirm that their account is not exact. Their significance lies in their answer to the second question: what is the nature, the essence of things that are.[1]

Again we have two groups, but this time not only holding alternative, if incompatible views, but overtly opposed to one another. They are linked in contest reminiscent of the battle of gods and giants; they are in fact the tender and the tough minded philosophers, characterized as gentle and violent respectively (246 C9, D1). Plato leaves no doubt on whose side his sympathies lie. Who are they?

The "giants" define being as the same thing as body, and they drag everything down to earth, as it were (246 A7 f.). Their adversaries, on the other hand, "cautiously defend their position somewhere in the heights of the unseen," maintaining that true being[2] consists in certain "intelligible and bodiless forms" (246 B).

The bodies of their opponents and what is called by them the truth ... They call not *ousia* but a moving process of *genesis* (becoming) (246 B9–C2).

---

[1] The "exact" philosophers also gave answers to the *poia*-question, viz. in terms of "hot," "cold," "wholeness" etc. But Plato did not consider them under that aspect, thinking perhaps that they had already come to grief over the question "how many?".

[2] Plato uses the term *ousia* rather than *on* in the present section, underscoring perhaps that his concern is intension, i.e., the essence of being.

They will later be referred to as "friends of the forms" (248 A4). Both groups escape, so it seems, the strictures against the two previous groups. They do not make being a substantial attribute (a) of a number of things, which involves a one/many problem, as in the case of the h and c philosophers, or (b) of one thing (on Plato's interpretation of Parmenides), which stands in need of further description and therefore has similar consequences. They locate being in one differentiating attribute[3] which is pervasive and universally descriptive: body (or as we might prefer to say, extension) on the one hand, the intelligible – note: not mind! – on the other. The implication is that what does not possess that attribute is not real, not *ontos on* but appearance or illusion. Thus the most radical among the giants

would hold out to the end that whatever they cannot squeeze between their hands is just nothing at all (247C5–7).

Traditionally the two parties have been called "materialists" and "idealists", and I have bowed to convention in adopting these names for the present section, although they do not strictly apply. Plato had as yet no concept of matter, and the most likely candidates for the "giants", Leucippus and Democritus are not materialists in the coarse sense here imputed; the atoms are intrinsically imperceptible and postulated *a priori*. The "idealists", the friends of the forms, on the other hand, must be the Plato of the middle period and perhaps a conservative wing among his disciples at the Academy. But again, the forms are not ideas in the mind (see p. 2 above), although admittedly they functioned as ideals. Be that as it may, differentiating attribute monists cannot be attacked by involving them in a one/many problem but need to be persuaded that their account is incomplete, that being must reasonably be ascribed to entities that do not possess the specified attribute. And this is what Plato is trying to do.

Turning to the materialists, the Stranger asks whether they must not admit any *onta* (things that possess being) which are bodiless. Souls cause them no difficulty; according to Leucippus these, too, are composed of atoms, albeit of spherical shape. But as far as wisdom and other virtues are concerned, the more civilized materialist will not have the courage either to deny their existence or to affirm that they are bodies, so that he is forced to admit that at least a small part of reality is bodiless (247 C9–D1). The Stranger then suggests that there must be

[3] They are "differentiating attribute monists"; on the substantial/differentiating attribute terminology see C. D. Broad (1937) c. 1.

a common character which may serve as a distinguishing mark (*horos*) of *ta onta* which both body and the bodiless possess. He proposes that

anything has real being (*ontos einai*) that is so constituted as to possess any sort of power (*dunamis*) either to affect anything else or to be affected, in however small a degree, by the most insignificant agent, even though it be only once (247D8–E3).[4]

The criterion may be acceptable to the materialists for want of a better, and in any case it covers tangibility, the mark implied in their own identification of being with the bodily – "what can be squeezed between their hands." But whatever their reaction, the materialists are not the Stranger's main target, and they now drop out.[5] The *dunamis* criterion is to help him lay bare the insufficiency of the account of being which the other party, the friends of the forms, and so Plato himself, had to offer.

But will it also make a positive contribution towards a more adequate account of the nature (the essence) of being? Its very careful and strikingly precise formulation seems to point in that direction. It looks as though Plato was here going to try out something new and exciting. And within limits this is certainly the case. On the other hand, there is also a sceptical note, for no sooner has the Stranger introduced his criterion than he foresees that he may perhaps later change his mind (247 E7 f.). And indeed, right at the beginning of the present section he seems to anticipate failure: once his investigation of earlier thinkers is completed, he says, we shall see that "being is no easier to define than not-being" (245 E8–246 A1). In fact, this result will be reaffirmed after both giants and gods have been done with when the Stranger will confess that "we are still in the dark about being" (249 E2–3).

---

[4] On power (*dunamis*) and its role in perception see Cornford (1935), pp. 234–239. The criterion probably originated with writers on medicine; cp. *Phaedr.* 270D.

[5] They are relatively unimportant in comparison with the idealists, similarly as in the preceding sections the h and c philosophers in comparison with Parmenides.

§ 10. Being, Forms and Motion: 248A–249D

This section may conveniently be introduced by recalling an earlier quotation regarding the position of the idealists (246 B9–C2):

The bodies of their opponents and what is called by them the truth ... they call not *ousia* but a moving process of *genesis* (becoming).

Accordingly the distinction between *ousia* and *genesis* as separate (*choris*) from one another forms the starting point of the present discussion. This is one of three contrasts already referred to, on which Plato's notion of being, as expressed in his classical *eidos* conception, had depended. The basic question is still "what is being?" But the argument now shifts to the cognition of being. What happens when we know being? When the Stranger offers his *dunamis* criterion – the power to affect and to be affected – to the friends of the forms (as he had put it to the other party) they are willing to accept it for "their communion with becoming by means of the body through sense"; and a corresponding account of sense perception had in fact been presented in the *Theaetetus*. But they do not accept it for "their communion with absolute being (*ontos ousia*) by means of the soul through reasoning" (248 A10 f., 248 C7–9). Why not?

Perhaps they might not object to *dunamis* as a purely ontological criterion, for earlier on in the dialogue the Stranger had used that very language, when he said that being might be "affected" by unity in virtue of its unitary parts (p. 27 above). But that affection would be a timeless, objective relation between being and unity, not involving process or change.[1] They oppose *dunamis* as a cognitive criterion in-

---

[1] 248C8–9 seems to cast doubt on the admissibility of *dunamis*, and therefore affection even as a characterisation of such purely ontological relations, unless it is the cognition of being which Plato had here in mind. In any case, in subsequent discussions of form/form relations he avoids "affection" using instead "participation" and kindred terms which he evidently did not consider as connoting power or affection.

There is therefore little plausibility in the view that Plato seeks the agreement of the

volving a subject and his soul. The Stranger goes on to enumerate five alternative ways in which *dunamis* might operate in the cognitive relation (248 D4–7). Substituting "active" for "affect," and "acted upon" for "affected," we get:

(1) Both subject and object are active.
(2) Both subject and object are acted upon.
(3) Both subject and object are active as well as acted upon.
(4) The subject is active and the object is acted upon.
(5) The object is active and the subject is acted upon.

We may note in passing that in the account of sense perception in the *Theaetetus* the first alternative was developed: both sense-object and sense-organ (the subject) are active in giving birth to the sensible quality.

When the Stranger in our passage puts the five alternatives to Theaetetus as possible characterizations of knowing, the latter thinks that neither of them is acceptable to the friends of the forms, since they would involve them in a contradiction. The Stranger interprets:

I see what you mean. They would have to say this: if knowing is to be active, it follows that what is known must be acted upon; and so, on this showing, being (*ousia*) when known by the act of knowledge must in so far as it is known be changed (*kineisthai*)[2] owing to being so acted upon; and that, we say, cannot happen to that which is changeless (248D10–E4).

We may note that of the five alternatives only one (no. 4) is considered, and that only as a supposal (cp. Ross, 1951, p. 110). Unlike the materialists, the idealists do not accept *dunamis* as characterizing the knowledge of being, although they need not, and surely would not, deny that the soul is active in seeking knowledge. Moreover the Stranger makes no attempt to convince them that they ought to accept his criterion by choosing alternatives (1) or (5) neither of which would *prima facie* involve them in a contradiction, i.e., force them to sacrifice the immutability of being, of the forms. In fact, at this point Plato seems to have lost interest in the criterion altogether, it disappears from the dialogue, not to be mentioned again. (He did predict, though, that he might perhaps change his mind – p. 32 above.)

idealists to the operation of *dunamis* in the cognition of forms *in order* that they may not object when he later expounds his doctrine of the mutual participation of forms, as Crombie (1963), p. 421 believes. Form-form relations are part of the eternal structure of reality, and therefore of an altogether different order from the mind-form, i.e. the cognitive relation.

[2] Literally "be moved." The corresponding noun *kinesis* – a key term in our dialogue – will in the sequel be rendered as "motion" or "movement" because we need the contrast with "rest" (*stasis*). The Greek term has however a much wider connotation than its English equivalents, referring to change in general as well as to change of place.

The argument now takes a different turn. The Stranger delivers what to all intents and purposes is a frontal attack against the position that being is changeless, i.e., against that Parmenidoid feature of the classical *eidos* conception which had not come under fire in his earlier argument with Parmenides (§ 8). Here is what he says:

> But tell me in heaven's name: are we really to be so easily convinced that motion (change), life, soul and understanding are not present to absolute being, that it has neither life nor thought, but stands immutable in solemn aloofness, devoid of intelligence? (248E6–249A2)

This poetic passage has been variously interpreted. At one time it was believed that forms are now to be credited with life and have souls. More sophisticated contemporary writers have thought that by affirming the consequent of the preceding hypothetical (that being cannot be changeless, which the idealists deny) the Stranger has also affirmed the antecedent (that knowing affects its object). Thus Runciman (1962) p. 81 f., assumes that Plato now holds that the forms, though having immutable characteristics – but surely, they *are* immutable characteristics! – are affected in being known. But Runciman does not succeed in showing in which sense forms are affected in being known, while yet remaining immutable. Nor do I find Moravcsic's answer – "Forms are subject to change and motion only in the sense that dated (temporal) propositions are true of them" (1962, p. 40) – helpful.[3] Surely the affection would have to be an ontological one, for the idealists would never deny that they are making true statements about forms.

In fact the Stranger will argue for quite different positions, two of them to be precise. After establishing that intelligence implies life, and both intelligence and life a soul, in which they reside, he asks:

> But then if it has intelligence, life and soul, can we say that a living being remains altogether immovable (changeless)? (249A9–10)

When this is dismissed by Theaetetus as unreasonable the Stranger draws his first conclusion:

A. In that case we must admit movement and what is moved as things which are (*onta*) (249B2–3).

---

[3] I fear that Moravcsic is thinking here of forms as concepts which undergo change and motion as they become subjects of predication. But our true *logoi* do not determine, not even affect, the structure of reality, they are determined by it (cp. § 1, p. 2 above and § 12, p. 48 below).

35

A does not affirm that being in its own nature moves or is moved, or that forms, as vehicles of being are moved, i.e. affected in being known.[4] All that is said is that motion and moving things have being (like the forms), and the moving things referred to at the moment are intelligence, life and soul. A is analogous to the admission extracted from the materialists. While the latter were persuaded to include some bodiless things, e.g., the virtues, among what is, the idealists must make their concession regarding motion and moving things.[5] As far as the nature of being is concerned the result is purely negative. The Stranger has considered the definitions put forward by the two parties and found them both too narrow.

The Stranger now returns to cognition and expands A by pointing out that both a completely changeless world (Parmenidean) and a world of total change (Heraclitean) would preclude the existence of intelligence. In the former, we may interpret, it would have no place, in the latter no objects. In other words, for anything to be a knower it must be in motion (engaging in dialogue, actual or silent), for anything to be known it must be unmoved.

Without rest [the Stranger continues] nothing that ever comes to be remains constant in the same condition and in the same respect, and again, without such objects intelligence could neither arise nor exist (249B12–C4).[6]

This leads to the final conclusion:

B. The philosopher must refuse to accept from the champions either of the one [Eleatics] or of the many forms [idealists] that the all (*to pan*) is changeless (at rest), and he must turn a deaf ear to those who represent being everywhere in motion [Heracliteans]. Like a child begging for both, he must

---

[4] Surely A follows from the immediately preceding sentence, put as a rhetorical question and quoted above (249A9–10), not from the discarded antecedent, twenty lines up (248D10 ff., p. 34, above), as Moravcsic suggests.

[5] Differentiating attribute monists, as pointed out (p. 31), need to be shown that their account is incomplete, that being must reasonably be ascribed to entities that do not possess the specified attribute. The attribute put forward on behalf of the friends of the forms was bodiless intelligibility. But this implied immutability and immobility, a position which will presently be reaffirmed. Now if moving things are included among *ta onta*, this must mean that things are included which *qua* moving are not intelligible. That things *qua* moving (changing) are refractory to intellection remains Plato's position, and for evidence we need not look back to the "objects of opinion" in the *Republic*. We can refer to *Soph.* 264A where perceptual judgments (which result from a "moving process of *genesis*") are classed as "appearance." Further, at *Phaedr.* 246A Socrates, after having defined the soul as self-moving mover, confesses his inability to tell us about, i.e. to describe its nature, offering a myth instead, and the "likely story" in the *Timaeus* (29C f.) is another case in point.

[6] Here Plato does not explicitly refer to forms but to things that come to be: i.e. changing things, which are said to be intelligible not *qua* moving but in virtue of, and in so far as they possess, permanent characteristics which in turn would be accounted for in terms of immovable forms in which they participate. By implication the passage refers to forms too.

declare that being or the sum total of things (*to on te kai to pan*) is both at once – all that is immovable (unchangeable) and all that is in motion (changeable) (249C10–D4).

Conclusion B confirms conclusion A but goes beyond it in two important respects.

(i) In agreement with the liberalization of the old hierarchical order of reality referred to repeatedly, not only motion, life, soul and intelligence but all moving things are included among *ta onta*, and this must mean the materialists' bodies as well.

(ii) B implies a distinction (which will come into full view in the next section, § 11) between the intension of being (*on, ousia, einai*) and its extension, the sum total of things that are (*to on kai pan*) – the universe. By insisting that being in the latter sense comprises both all things immovable and all things in motion, being in the former sense can no longer be conceived in terms of the immovable/movable contrast, i.e., the intension of being has now been differentiated from the Parmenidoid form. The conceptual symbiosis of *eide* and being has been dissolved, and being can no longer be defined in terms of the forms. They have ceased to be its exclusive vehicle.

Nothing that has been said in these passages precludes that some things may be sometimes at rest and sometimes in motion, or at rest in some respects and in motion in others. On the other hand, what has been said does not imply that all things must be both at rest and in motion, or at rest in some respects and in motion in others at the same time.[7] Nor does it imply that there are not some things which are always at rest (e.g. forms), and others which are always in motion (e.g. souls, rivers, data of sense).

Among commentators, Moravcsic, arguing against Ross, has complained that the passage offers "no sustained argument," unless we grant that it established that forms, too, are subject to motion and change, if only in the emaciated (and un-Platonic) sense quoted earlier (p. 35 above). He cannot understand why the *dunamis* criterion should have been dropped without rhyme or reason after having been introduced with so much care and circumspection. Nor would he think that A and B are worth-while conclusions if they only established, in addition to forms, the existence of souls in whose reality Plato had believed anyhow.

---

[7] This seems to be Moravcsic's (1962) surely erroneous reading of B when he interprets: "what exists is in motion and not in motion" (p. 40), "an existent must be characterized as being in a sense in motion and being in some sense at rest" (p. 41).

Beginning with the last point, we grant that Plato always believed in the reality of the soul. But since forms were the vehicles of being, and souls *qua* moving were not forms, their ontological status had been left in doubt. Further, being is now accorded, not only to souls but to all things movable, and here we have an obvious parallel with the concessions extracted from the materialists. Lastly, there is a further parallel with the earlier discussion of the monists (Parmenides) (§ 8), in so far as on both occasions we have been able to discern a significant development in Plato's ontological thinking. So far then our passage has its place in the coherent development of Plato's arguments.

There is, it is true, a break at 248 E6 (p. 35 above) when the *dunamis* criterion disappears from sight, and the Stranger's language suddenly assumes a poetic and passionate character (Crombie: "a rhetorical outburst"?). These two features should make us pause and we should certainly not try to argue them away. They seem to indicate Plato had reached a point where a change of direction had become necessary. How so?

I can think of two considerations which may have been in his mind:

(1) Plato may have toyed with the idea of applying the *dunamis* criterion, so successful in accounting for perception, to intellectual cognition, all the more so as he expressed the epistemic relation in both cases by the same term as a *koinonia* (communion). He may have hoped to rid his *eidos* conception of its last Parmenidoid feature, *akineton* (motionless), but then got worried and withdrew, lest he might lead his students into the trap of Protagorean relativism.[8]

(2) Secondly, Plato, sustained thinker that he was, may have realized that he was in duty bound to consider the other alternatives of the *dunamis* operation as well, in particular alternatives (1) and (5) (see p. 34 above). But if so, his idealist diehards might have carried the day, and he would have missed his chance of convincing them that motion and moving things are just as much part of reality as the immutable forms. The only way to enlist their support was to remind them of their soul, the moving thing *par excellence*, and yet the indispensable correlate of the immutable forms.

So much then for the giants and the gods.

---

[8] For references to passages in the *Timaeus* and *Philebus* where Plato continued to maintain his belief in immutable forms, see Ross (1951), p. 110.

Appendix

The above paper was originally presented to the International Philosophical Congress at Brussels in 1953, and has recently been reissued (de Vogel, 1970, ch. VIII) together with some reconsiderations (*ibid.*, ch. IX, pp. 194–209). In the context of the passage we have been considering (§ 10) I would concur with the author in giving an affirmative answer to her question, viz. on the ground that Plato will presently introduce a form of motion as one of his very great kinds. (The conceptual difficulties which a form of motion raises for Plato will be discussed in subsequent sections *passim*.) There is similar agreement to the effect that whatever follows from our passage, it does not imply that forms are moved. Further, although it is my view that in this passage Plato works up to a distinction between the intension and the extension of being, at 249 A1 the distinction has not yet been made. *To pantelos on* (absolute being) does not refer to the totality of things, is not equivalent to *to on te kai to pan*. What does it refer to?

In the section of the *Sophist* beginning at 242 B, of which our passage forms part, Plato is searching for a definition of being, and the notion under attack is still the Eleatic *estin* in so far as it had been appropriated by the Idealists, and so by Plato himself, to their Parmenidoid forms. The emphasis then is on "being" (the form of being), and the question at issue is "does being move?". And it must move if it possesses soul (the self-moving mover) and intellect. The answer that will emerge from our dialogue is a clear "no." Being can be predicated of motion but not motion of being (p. 42 f.).

On the face of it this conclusion seems to be at variance with the Stranger's remarks from 248 E6 to 249 A10. But it may be noted that these remarks are put as questions, and although Theaetetus answers them in the affirmative, no affirmative conclusion is drawn by the Stranger. The only conclusions he draws are those I have listed under A (249 B 2 f.) and B (249 C10–D4).

De Vogel, on the other hand, pointing to parallels between our passage and the *Timaeus*, argues that *to pantelos on* can be understood by reference to *to panteles zoon* of the latter work, the archetypal living creature which serves as the demiurge's model for the visible cosmos. She takes *to pantelos on* as referring to the intelligible world in its totality, holding that this totality appeared to Plato as an articulate unity, since it can be exhibited by dialectic, and that an articulate unity presupposes an organic unity. Thus supplementing whatever force the Stranger's questions from 248 E6 to 249 A10 may have, she concludes that Plato has here conceived of the intelligible world of forms as a living world, possessed of soul and intellect. With this conclusion I cannot concur.

Without going into the question of the relative dates of the two dialogues, it seems plausible that some of the notions put forward in the *Timaeus* were present to Plato's mind when he wrote the *Sophist* (see e.g. references to divine craftsmanship at 265 C ff.) and vice versa. Yet I feel that the doctrines of each dialogue should be appraised in their own context. The *Timaeus* is a work on cosmology, which is not an issue in the *Sophist* which is concerned with being and not-being, and in our passage in particular with a conceptual differentiation of being from the forms at large. Thus seen, it seems highly unlikely that at this point absolute or perfect being (*to pantelos on*) should stand for the intelligible world of the "friends of the forms." Nor does Plato in our passage assert that the "intelligible and bodiless forms" in which they believe form a unity, let alone an organic unity; the term *zoon* does not occur.

But even in the *Timaeus* Plato does not affirm that the prototypal creature possesses motion, life, soul or intellect; for then it would change, while the demiurge looks for his model to the eternal which is always in the same state (29 A). I would agree with Cornford (1937) p. 40 that the prototypal creature is not itself a living creature, any more than the form of man is a man. Consequently, in fashioning the world-soul the demiurge does not turn to the *panteles zoon* but uses the very great kinds of the *Sophist* as his elements, that is being, sameness and difference. As far as motion is concerned the created soul, in accordance with the *Phaedrus* doctrine, possesses it all by herself (37 A).

Next, at 39 E Plato enumerates four intelligible forms of living creatures that are contained in the prototype: the traditional gods and the three types of natural kinds (winged, water- and land-animals). He does not enumerate any other forms. As Cornford (*ibid.*, p. 40) points out, "the intelligible living creature is a generic form which contains in itself the forms of all the subordinate species . . .". Consequently it is not, sotospeak, in the same category as the "being" which is at stake throughout the *Sophist*. In the language of this dialogue, it would participate in being, but being does not participate in it.

Finally a word concerning conclusion B (249 C10 ff., p. 36 above) where I concur with Ross in taking *kekinemena* as referring to all things in motion including the materialists' bodies which come to be and pass away. De Vogel, on the other hand, would reserve the term to souls and intelligence, i.e. to spiritual motion, arguing that Plato right down to the *Timaeus* and *Philebus* never gave up his basic distinction between being and becoming. Quite so! But in our *Sophist* passage (B) neither *akineta* nor *kekinemena* are considered as vehicles of being. They are considered as part of *to on te kai to pan*, that is as constituting the extension of being (compare pp. 37 and 41). The move which Plato has made at this point accords well with the general trend in the *Sophist* to allow for things to have real being as what they are (see § 5). Admittedly, Plato might have claimed that this "liberalization" was forced upon him because in order to unmask the Sophist's stratagem he had to show that even semblances and falsehoods are "really and truly" what they are.

§ 11. Can we define Being?: 249D–251A

Plato has now completed his survey of accounts of being by previous (and contemporary) philosophers, but as anticipated, it has not yielded a definition (*logos*) of being. It is at this point that the Stranger confesses that he is still in the dark about being (249 E2–3). The discussion which now follows hinges on the distinction between the intension and the extension of being (cp. p. 37 above). In referring to the former Plato speaks of being "according to its own nature" (*kata ten hautou phusin* – 250 C6), and regarding the latter he speaks of the all (*to pan*) or the sum total of things (*to on kai pan*). Things *are* because they are "encompassed" or "encircled" by being (*periechein* – 250 B8), a term with a long tradition in philosophy from Anaximander onwards. Here it gives us the extension of being (*to on*) which we should express by drawing a circle, inside which we place the things which are (*ta onta*), i.e. we literally encircle them. We meet the same term again later in the dialogue in precisely the same sense: In the section on dialectic we shall hear of "forms encircled from without by one form" (253 D7 f., p. 53 below).

In the present passage Plato, who lacks our technical vocabulary, is engaged in working out this distinction as though making it clear to himself. Referring to his earlier conclusion that the sum of things is all that is at rest and all that is in motion, the Stranger is wondering whether he has not laid himself open to the very questions which he had put to the h and c philosophers when they contended that the hot and the cold *are* all things. What then is the relation between motion, rest and being? His argument can conveniently be set out in four steps.

1. Motion and rest are things "most opposed" to one another (250 A8 f.). We need to add here the words "according to their own nature," and we may interpret "most opposed to one another" as "incompatible

with one another." This point will prove to be of considerable importance as we go along.[1]

2. Motion and rest both and severally *are* (250 A11 f.). But when we say this, we do not mean that they both are in motion or both are at rest (250 B2–6), for they are incompatible.[2]

3. Therefore being, according to its own nature, cannot be motion or rest or both, but must be something other, a third thing, although being in *extenso* comprises both, for they both *are* (250 B7 ff.). This, as we have seen, is expressed by the formula that they are encircled by being, and in this sense, do they have communion (*koinonia*) with being.

4. In virtue of its own nature, being is neither at rest nor in motion (250 C6 f.); this result has been half anticipated by the carefully worded conclusions A and B in § 10, which were explicitly restricted to the extension of being.

I think we have no reason to object to Plato's argument (contra Moravcsic 1962, p. 28n. cp. Runciman, 1962, p. 94), as long as we take note of the two senses of being which are involved, and which Plato is here elaborating. What is distinct from motion and rest is the intension, not the extension of being. The latter allows us to predicate being of both motion and rest – in itself no mean achievement in the face of idealist opposition – but this does not entitle us to predicate motion or rest of being, for such predication would affect being according to its own nature, i.e. its intension.

What, then, is the nature of being? Plato cannot tell. The question "what is being?" remains unanswered.

But surely, what does not move must be at rest and what is not at rest must move, i.e. everything must either move or be at rest. Yet being neither moves nor does not move; that is to say, in its own nature, it is neither Heraclitean nor Parmenidean. It lies outside these alternatives (250 C12–D2). Plato seems to imply, though he does not say in so many words, that since anything specific is either at rest or in motion, no specific property whatever must be ascribed to being. The Stranger recalls the difficulty which we experienced earlier concerning

---

[1] Incompatibility entails (a) that motion and rest cannot participate in one another, and (b) that the same thing cannot participate in both motion and rest at the same time and in the same respect.

[2] This seems to imply self-predication – motion is in motion, rest is at rest. But how else could Plato state their descriptive content? To move or to be moved must be of the nature of motion, and to be at rest of the nature of rest. And we need the mention of both, for it is in virtue of their natures – true, the natures which they are – that they are incompatible.

not-being, when we were asked, to what that name could be applied (250 D7 f., cp. § 4) and confesses to be now in no less a perplexity with regard to being. His criticisms of Parmenides seem to have come back to him with a vengeance.

A significant difference concerning being and not-being must however be noted. While absolute not-being was seen to be both non-descriptive and non-referring, being, though non-descriptive, does refer, namely to all the things that are, including motion and rest. They are encompassed by being and in this sense share in being.

Being, so it seems, will turn out a purely formal notion, that is to say, a form of a higher order, a form of forms, as it were. Since we cannot, as Plato at one time thought, attribute any differentiating characteristic to it, e.g. immovable, it must be intrinsically indefinable.[3] The Stranger concludes on a hopeful note though: since we are now equally perplexed about being and not-being, any light we may be able to shed on one will perhaps also enlighten us on the other.[4]

[3] Moravcsic (1962, *passim*) makes the point that being is "topic neutral", which does not quite come to the same thing. Being in the *Sophist* is still counted among the *eide* or *gene* (forms, kinds), to wit the very great ones. I would reserve "topic neutral" for participation and kindred terms, which do not stand for forms, i.e. are not ontological designates within Plato's philosophy.

[4] This hope will be fulfilled; see p. 68 below. On the importance of the joint illumination compare Owen (1970) p. 229 f., whose essay only came to my notice after the present study had been substantially completed.

§ 12. The Communion of Forms and the "Late Learners": 251A–252E

As we approach the central doctrines of the dialogue it may be as well to recall briefly how we got to the point at which we now find ourselves. We began by searching for a definition of the Sophist. We seemed to be pretty close to it when we discerned him as an arch-deceiver, a fabricator of semblances and falsehoods. But at that stage he met us with the puzzle that no statement can be false; for to say what is false is to say what is-not, and what is-not, *pace* Parmenides, can neither be thought nor be uttered, so that all statements must be true. Thus it became necessary to challenge Parmenides' canon. In order to tackle the Sophist we must show

that what is-not, in some sense *is* and that, on the other hand, what is, in a way is-not (241 D5–7, p. 21 above).

We must establish that there is *symploke*, an inter-weaving of being and not-being, and it is with this end in view that Plato will now develop his doctrine of the combination of forms.

But the Sophist is a cunning animal, lying in wait for us with a fresh stratagem at every corner. So he will now present us with a second puzzle, likewise rooted in Parmenides, extending the latter's doctrine that there is nothing besides being (fr. VIII, 36 f.) to the subject of every sentence. This puzzle in a sense cuts even more deeply than the former, because it restricts the possibility of stating anything to the utterance of tautologies, that is to a level of discourse at which no information, either true or false, can be conveyed. According to this doctrine, you cannot call the same thing by several names, you can only call it by one name; otherwise you would affirm of it what it is-not. One thing cannot be many. You can only speak of a man as man, and of a good as good, but not of a man as good (251 B9–C2). And this once again, is a logical veto. The philosophers who delight in this sort of

44

game,[1] young men as well as elderly ones who have come to learning late in life, present an inverted epitome, as it were, of Plato's own criticisms of Parmenides. Was Parmenides not told that he was not entitled to attribute anything whatever to his one being, nay not even give it one name? And is this not also Plato's implied criticism of his own Parmenidoid forms, as he began to discover their inner complexity as wholes of parts, participating in both the one and the many?

The introduction of these "late learners" seems highly relevant at a point in the dialogue, when Plato has only just freed himself from the Eleatic spell, and is about to establish that forms can combine with one another. For this must mean that each form will receive many attributions, and thus be called by several names.[2] These people, however, would tell him that he is trying to do the logically impossible. Hence the arguments that follow will be addressed not only to those with whom we have been conversing earlier, but to these "late learners" as well (251 C8–D2).

The Stranger now raises the crucial question of the combination of forms. In the present section he does not explicitly speak of "forms" or "kinds", as he will in the sequel. He refers to motion, rest and being, as well as to some of the other notions which he had considered in his arguments with previous philosophers, and he speaks indefinitely of "things". That forms are his subject-matter will become obvious in the next section. We need hardly repeat, though, that the form conception that is to emerge from the ensuing discussions will be altogether different from the one we knew in the middle dialogues.

Plato uses a variety of terms to express the relations which forms have with one another.[3] But none of these should be looked upon as philosophical terms in an exclusively technical sense, though they acquire technical status when applied to form/form relations.[4] Three

---

[1] The doctrine has traditionally been identified with Antisthenes, but see now Guthrie (1969), p. 216 f.

[2] I disagree with Cornford (1935), p. 253 who thought the question how a thing can have many names is a merely trivial one, since it was solved long ago by the theory of ideas. It may be a trivial one, as far as attributions to particulars are concerned, though only on the assumption that the theory as originally conceived, survived the criticisms of *Parm.* pt. I. But even if that was Plato's position at the time he wrote the *Sophist*, the question is still not a trivial one as far as forms are concerned. For whether there are any relations between forms, which allow us to make attributions to them (to call them by several names) is stated as a problem awaiting solution at *Parm.* 129 D–E, and the answer is to be given now.

[3] For a useful survey of these terms see Lorenz and Mittelstrass (1966), p. 131, n. 60.

[4] I shall abbreviate: f = form, p = particular; accordingly I shall speak of f/f, p/f, and p/p relations.

groups of terms seem especially important. The first is *koinonia* (communion, combination) and derivative nouns and verbs. We had met this term before in connection with the idealists where it was used to express epistemological relations (§ 10). The second group of words connotes mingling and blending, and a third participation and sharing (*metechein, metalambanein*). The two latter terms had been most frequently used in the middle dialogues to express the p/f relation. But it must not be overlooked that there is a categorical distinction between f/f and p/f relations. Thus "motion and rest participate in being" is not equivalent to "all moving things participate in being and all things at rest participate in being," though the latter is certainly also the case (§ 10). Nor would it be correct to render an f/f relation as a generalised p/p relation, e.g. "motion participates in being" = "all cases of motion are cases of being." Platonic forms, according to their own nature, are not classes of particulars, and consequently f/f relations are not reducible to relations involving particulars. The liberalisation which has taken place in the *Sophist* allows us to fill the "circle" of being with the forms of motion and rest, as well as with all the things that are in motion or at rest, but the categorical boundary between forms and particular things has thereby not been obliterated.

In this and the following sections we are only concerned with relations of forms, and while it is true that these determine the relations in which particulars may stand, the significance of the former is not exhausted by the latter. In this respect Plato has not budged. On the other hand, he seems willing to accept the possibility or impossibility of certain relations concerning particulars as a negative criterion for his ontological analysis.[5]

Cornford (1935) p. 256 f. held that all f/f relations are symmetrical relations, and has been severely taken to task for his view by practically everybody. He seems to have been guided by the consideration that for Plato f/f relations are intensional, i.e. pure meaning relations, and not, as for Aristotle, relations between classes of particulars. This much at least is evident from his comments (p. 270 f.) as well as from his diagrams with their overlapping shadings (pp. 271, 278). While I have much sympathy with his position, I feel that f/f relations are not sufficiently differentiated in Plato to be taken in a purely intensional, let alone a strictly extensional sense. I have tried to trace some of the complexities with which we are faced in the relations of motion and

---

[5] For an example see p. 49 below. For another "negative" criterion see p. 48 f.

rest with being, relations which, as we have seen (§ 11), are certainly *not* symmetrical. But, anticipating later argument, I want to say now, in defence of Cornford, that some of the most important f/f relations with which we shall be concerned, will turn out to be symmetrical relations (see p. 86 below).

If Cornford erred on the side of intension, Ackrill (1957) has gone too far in the opposite direction. He seems to mistake f/f relations, as exemplified in Platonic divisions, for Aristotelian classifications. His example is

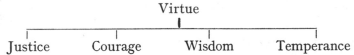

This no doubt is a neat schema to accommodate a traditional Greek view but ignores the intension of the terms thus arranged. If we reflect for a moment on the Socratic/Platonic doctrine that the virtues are one (*Prot.* 329 C ff.), that virtue is essentially a sort of wisdom (e.g. *Meno* 88 C f., cp. *Phaedo* 69A), and similarly courage, we shall find ourselves at once in a maze of cross-divisions.

Ross (1951) p. 111 n. 6 had drawn attention to the fact that Plato used "communion" words sometimes in a dative, sometimes in a genitive construction. Ackrill (1957) seemed right in pointing out that the former expresses a general unspecified relation, and I would agree that the latter stands for a definite and specific one. Again Ackrill went too far in claiming that the genitive construction expresses the fact that one concept *falls under* another (p. 217).[6] Motion and rest are not subsumed under being as two species of a genus, or as instances of a universal.

The Stranger considers three possible alternatives concerning the combination of forms: (i) no form combines with any other form, (ii) every form combines with every other form, (iii) some forms combine with one another, and some do not.

(i) The first alternative seems closely linked with the puzzle served up by the "late learners." If we are only allowed to utter identical statements then we should have no means of expressing a combination of forms. We could not say, as we have just done, that motion and rest have a share in being. Indeed the whole history of philosophy down to

---

[6] On forms as concepts, see § 1, p. 2 above.

Plato's own day would stand condemned, insofar as its doctrines had been expressed in synthetic statements.

This, however, is not the Stranger's approach. Leaving the "late learners" on one side for a moment, he argues that, unless forms did combine, our statements concerning the relations of motion and rest etc., would be meaningless. No philosopher who attached being or unity or motion or rest to anything would have talked sense ("said anything") if there was no mingling between the entities referred to (252 B5 f.).

It is obvious that ontological relations are here considered as logically prior to our statements about them. And it is on these terms that the Stranger now refers to the "late learners",

who will not allow one thing to share in the quality of another, and so be called by its name (252 B9–10).

In other words he takes their linguistic veto to be based on an onto-logical presupposition.[7] And he turns the tables on them by pointing out that the very language they use is incompatible with their thesis:

In speaking of anything they are obliged to use the words "to be", "apart", "from the others", "by itself" and countless others (252C2–4),

i.e. they cannot but combine, and express themselves in synthetic statements. Their practice belies their theory, which is branded as absurd and duly made fun of.

The linguistic practice of the "late learners" which the Stranger has in mind seems to be common-sense talk ("speaking of anything") rather than the enunciation of their own theory, though it would apply to that as well. But the examples which he gives are curiously loaded. They are reminiscent of the terminology of the friends of Parmenidoid forms. It therefore looks as though he wanted to kill two birds with one stone, and this is not all that farfetched, given the common Eleatic roots (to which we have referred repeatedly) of both the theory of ideas and the Sophists' capers. They are close cousins.

Plato has not established that there must be a combination of forms, he has shown that to deny this is inconsistent with the discourse we have. He seems to recognize that the expressions which a philosopher is compelled to use in expounding a theory are a negative criterion for

---

[7] In Mr. Moravcsic's terminology, Plato's view here is that semantic atomism implies ontological atomism, not the other way round; cp. Moravcsic (1962), p. 59.

its validity (see p. 46, n. 5). But the theory is logically prior to whatever expressions he uses in stating it.

(ii) The second alternative that all forms are capable of combining with one another is refuted by reference to the incompatibility of motion and rest, asserted earlier (250 A8 f., p. 41 f. above). Here Plato argues through the mouth of Theaetetus that if they were so capable

then motion itself would come completely (*pantapasin*) to rest, and rest itself would in turn be in motion, if they should supervene upon one another (252 D6–8).

The Stranger answers with a rhetorical question:

And this at least is absolutely [literally: with the greatest necessity] impossible that motion should come to be at rest and rest be in motion? (252 D9–10).

Theaetetus assents.

Once again self-predication, if not outright asserted, seems implied. If motion itself cannot be at rest, we are entitled to infer that this must be so, because it moves, and the same *mutatis mutandis* would hold regarding rest itself. As pointed out earlier (p. 42, n. 2), this ascription of movement to motion, and of being at rest to rest is the only means at Plato's disposal to describe their respective natures (apart from naming them). It is, of course, in virtue of their natures that they are incompatible, and indeed it is only *as* their respective natures that they are (cp. p. 69 below).

We might be tempted to say that their incompatibility depends on a hidden premise, viz. that a thing cannot be both in motion and at rest at the same time, and that it must be either in motion or at rest at any time.[8] Plato would rejoin that these facts about things are due to the natures of motion itself and rest itself, and that the latter are not distilled out of those facts. On the other hand, he might admit the latter as a negative criterion against anyone wishing to affirm that motion itself and rest itself can combine.[9] In fine, that the natures of motion and rest are recognizable in the behaviour patterns of things does not for Plato affect their *a priori* character.

Runciman (1962) p. 95 f., in a subtle and cautious argument, considers the possibility that in the present passage Plato merely wishes

---

[8] Leaving out of consideration for the purpose of this argument that a thing may at the same time be in motion in some respects and at rest in others.

[9] This is the first of the two criteria, referred to on p. 46 above.

to show (1) the non-identity of motion and rest,[10] and/or (ii) that motion and rest are not entirely (*pantapasin* 252 D6, p. 49 above) predicable of one another. There are several considerations which may favour such a weaker interpretation:

(a) on the view that forms are at rest *qua* knowable and in motion *qua* being known, it would appear that there is some communion between motion and rest, so that Plato might be anxious to affirm that there can not be total intercommunion between forms such as might obliterate their respective identities altogether.

(b) At 256 B6–7 there is a hypothetical suggestion that motion may somehow participate in rest.

I shall deal with (b) as a separate issue, when we come to the passage in question and here only wish to anticipate that it is inconclusive (see § 18 below). Regarding the other suggestion (a) made earlier, that forms *qua* being known are moved, I refer to § 10, pp. 35 f., 37 ff. above. The present passage should not be read in the light of that suggestion. On the contrary, the very strong wording with which the communion of motion and rest is now denied – as with the greatest necessity impossible (*megistais anagkais adunaton*) – lends added support to the view that Plato does not accept the changeability of objects of knowledge.

Predicability, as we have seen, is dependent on ontological relations. If it be held that motion and rest are "not entirely predicable of one another," this could only be so because they do not participate entirely, i.e. participate partially, in one another. But partial participation or degrees of participation would seem inconceivable to Plato, for whom participation is an all or nothing relation. Moreover, the three alternatives of f/f relations, which are here under consideration, leave no room for partial participation, and it seems that "not entirely predicable" is too diffuse a notion to be made good.

Some interpreters have held that since Plato will eventually break down the dichotomy, and therefore the incompatibility, of being and not-being he does *a fortiori* dispense with all incompatibilities, and so also with that of motion and rest. But the compatibility of being and not-being which Plato will be able to affirm is due to his discovery of the true nature of not-being, while it is the natures of motion and rest which render them incompatible. The attempt to force Plato into the position that there are no incompatibilities whatsoever, only non-

---

[10] This would hardly seem necessary, though, after what was said at 250 A8 (p. 41 above).

identities (which would have radical moral implications quite unacceptable to him) finds no support in this or later dialogues.

There is, however, a genuine difficulty for Plato with which he does not appear to have come to grips. If forms (*qua* objects of knowledge) are at rest, then the form of motion in its own nature (*qua* moving) cannot be known.[11] But an intrinsically unknowable form is a *contradictio in adjecto*. The answer would have to be that motion itself, after all, does *not* move. But then Plato would be hard put to account for the nature of motion and its incompatibility with rest. (See further discussion p. 71 and § 18 below).

(iii) The Stranger concludes by remarking that

one of the three alternatives [which he had proposed] must necessarily be true. Either all (forms) will blend, or none, or some will and some will not (252 E1–2).

Since the first two alternatives have been found impossible, the third must be affirmed. It wins by elimination but is not "necessarily true". From the Stranger's precise and unambiguous statement we may once again note that he leaves no room for partial blending.

[11] Compare the sensitive remarks by John Malcolm (1967) p. 141.

§ 13. Dialectic and Meta-dialectic: 252E–254B

The Stranger now introduces two analogies for his conclusion that some forms combine and some do not. The first analogy is with the letters of the alphabet, the second with musical sounds. In both cases an art (*techne*) is needed to discern which letters or sounds can combine with which: the art of the grammarian and of the musician respectively. The letter analogy (which occurs elsewhere in Plato) is particularly fruitful because of its distinction between vowels and consonants. It is the vowels that hold a special place in so far as they make the combination of letters (into words) possible:

The vowels more than the others are a sort of bond pervading them all, so that without a vowel the other letters cannot be joined to one another (253 A4–6).

The suggestion here is that there are certain all-pervading forms which are a sort of bond for other forms, and make their combinations possible. We shall see in due course which forms are candidates for that function; being will be one of them.

The art which is concerned with the combination of forms is called dialectic. Like the musician and the grammarian in the world of sounds and letters, so the dialectician recognizes and sets out combinations in the nature of things; they are not of his making. His work, as we know from *Phaedr.* 265 D f. comprises the complementary methods of collection and division, and it proceeds by noting precisely the degree of similarity and dissimilarity between things (*Phaedr.* 262A), avoiding to take the same form for another or vice versa (*Sophist* 253 D2). He divides according to kinds (253 D1) at the natural joints (*Phaedr.* 265 E). Division is no doubt the most important aspect of his work. It was profusely illustrated in the first part of our dialogue (218 D–236 C, p. 12 above), and will again be used by the Stranger when he offers his final definition of the Sophist at the end.

Two points may be noted in passing. Firstly, the dialectician does not impose a conceptual scheme on his material, but discerns and formulates its ontological structure.[1] That structure, as we noted in the preceding section, is in every sense prior to his exposition of it, i.e., *on* is prior to *logoi*. Secondly, will he not need intuition (*noësis*) as well in order to discern similarities and differences and isolate individual forms?

Plato gives two accounts of the science of dialectic in fairly close succession, and it may be convenient to set these out side by side, as follows:

A	B
(i) ... pointing out which kinds harmonize with which, and which reject (i.e. are incompatible with) one another;	The man who can do that discerns clearly
	(i) one form everywhere extended throughout many (particulars), each of which lies apart, and
(ii) also whether there are certain kinds that pervade them all and hold them together so that they can blend;	(ii) many forms different from one another encircled from without by one form;[3]
(iii) and again in divisions whether there are others that traverse wholes[2] and are responsible for the separation (253 B10–C3).	(iii) and again one form connected in unity through many wholes[2]
	(iv) and many forms entirely apart and separate.
	(v) This means knowing how to distinguish kind by kind, in what way the several kinds can or cannot combine (253 D5–E2).

A is a general account of the "art" (corresponding to grammar and music), which is needed in order to show which forms combine, and which do not; it is now called a science (*episteme*). It is only after A has been stated that the science is identified as dialectic (253 D3). In contrast to A, B is a much more detailed account of the work actually performed by the dialectician. It begins with collection (i), and in (ii) and (iii) spells out the nature of a complex division in both its extensional and intensional aspects; (iv) in particular shows how much Plato has his eye on the practice of division. It is the dialectician's business to explore a definite area such as, e.g., the nature of the Sophist. Consequently, at each stage one form will be singled out for further division, while others, which are not relevant to the purpose in hand, will remain "apart and separate", and not be further explored. (v) is

[1] Cp. Runciman (1962) p. 60.
[2] On "wholes" see p. 29 above.
[3] On "encircled from without" see p. 41 above.

more general again, summing up the gist of the work done. Thus B presents us with a fairly complete, if concise account of the dialectician's task, and once again Plato's didactic aims are apparent.

If B is concerned with work and practice, A gives us some of the foundations of dialectic. (i) is not only another clear indication that Plato in preceding arguments about motion and rest has been concerned with incompatibility, it recognizes incompatibility as a principle of his science. Further the words which we have rendered as "so that ... can" in (ii), and as "responsible" in (iii) point to the "vowel" function of certain kinds in so far as these make combinations and divisions possible, that is to say, such combinations and divisions as form the substance of B. Like the vowels, these kinds are all-pervasive and "a sort of bond."[4] A is more fundamental than B. While the subject-matter of B is dialectic proper, that of A can aptly be designated as meta-dialectic.[5]

This distinction, though not drawn by Plato in so many words, is important for our understanding of the sections that follow. We shall still be concerned with the combination of kinds and forms, but the discussion will be conducted at the meta-dialectical level, and accordingly the methods of collection and division will not be employed.

---

[4] This will even turn out to be true of the "kind" which is responsible for divisions, see p. 64 f. below.
[5] The Stranger's choice of terminology seems to underscore this distinction. While *genos* and *eidos* are often used indiscriminately of the Platonic form, *genos* is more general in connotation and *eidos* more specific. Accordingly we find *genos* exclusively used in A, and *eidos* exclusively in B (i)–(iv); in B (v) *genos* recurs, but this, as pointed out, is a generalized summary of the results of (i) to (iv).

§ 14. The very great Kinds – Introduction: 254B–D

The Stranger now picks up the thread from 252E (end of § 12), expanding the conclusion then reached in the light of what we have since learned about dialectic and meta-dialectic:

... some of the kinds will combine with one another, and some will not, some with a few and some with many, while some pervade all, and there is nothing against their being combined with everything (254 B7–C1).

We may notice that the impossibility of some combinations is again affirmed. On the other hand, that some will combine with a few, some with many is a new point, not previously argued for; it does not contribute to the arguments that follow. The last clause must be taken to refer to those kinds which are all-pervasive and make combinations and separations possible.

Having adumbrated the position reached, the Stranger indicates how we are to proceed in order to grasp being and not-being with such precision as may be possible, and see whether we can affirm that not-being *really* is not-being without falling into contradiction ("and remain unscathed," 254 D1–2). To this end,

we shall investigate not all forms, lest we get confused by their multitude, but select some of those that are recognized as very great, and first enquire into their respective natures and then into their capacity to combine with one another (254 C2–5).

The very great kinds (*megista gene*) which the Stranger will select are being, sameness (the same), difference (the other),[1] and motion and rest. The first three belong to those referred to in A (p. 53 above), i.e. they perform a "vowel" function and pervade all other kinds and forms as a sort of bond, "holding them together and traversing them" respectively.

---

[1] On sameness and difference see p. 27 n. 5 above.

The choice of the term *megista gene* testifies to some recognition on the part of Plato that he is here concerned with foundations, i.e., with what I wish to call a meta-enquiry. He has not the vocabulary available to express the logical priority that is involved, though he has indicated it, clearly enough for twentieth century ears, in terms of "all-pervasive," of "making possible" and "being responsible," and by invoking as an analogy the special function of vowels with regard to the other letters of the alphabet. Still, for Plato "being" etc. are superlative things – "very great" – among other things (cp. p. 22 n. 2 above), and there remains a lingering suspicion that he conceived of categorical distinctions as a matter of degree.[2] He has not drawn a sufficiently sharp line between the nature of his own philosophical enquiry and the philosophical method he teaches others. He will go on using *genos* and *eidos* synonymously, and I feel no compunction – after having drawn attention to their distinct usages in two key passages (p. 54 n. 5 above) – in following him, and in subsequent sections shall speak indifferently of "kinds" or "forms" of being, sameness, difference etc.

In any case, the term *genos* must not mislead us into assuming that the relation between the *megista gene* and the forms at large is a genus/species relation.[3] This were to read Aristotle back into Plato's terminology. The forms at large, the *eide* are indeed more specific than being, sameness and difference, in so far as they have descriptive content, standing for determinate natures, e.g. beauty, wisdom. Being, sameness and difference, though Plato speaks of their natures (*poia*), are purely formal determinants. Specific *eide* are known intuitively as what they are, and discursively in their relationship with other *eide*, i.e. by means of dialectic in the strict sense. The three *megista gene*, on the other hand, have no whatness. They are known in terms of their interrelations with one another, and depending on these, in terms of their "vowel" functions in the world of forms at large. Thus they can be understood in terms of the possibility of combinations and divisions which they provide, i.e. as the formal characterisations of substantive discursive knowledge. As pointed out earlier, they are forms of the (Platonic) forms, or meta-forms for short, and the study of their interrelations is meta-dialectic. It will be as a result of our meta-dialectical arguments, that we shall eventually be able to establish the *symploke* of being and not-being which is our goal.

2 Crombie (1963) p. 412: "One wonders in fact whether Plato did not mistakenly think that being *all*-pervasive is merely a matter of being *more* pervasive than highly generic properties such as being an animal."

3 cp. Gilbert Ryle (1966), p. 140.

But in spite of their purely formal "nature", and absence of whatness, the *megista gene*, these superlative things, do not cease for Plato to be ontological constituents. In this respect they are indeed like the vowels of the alphabet, which not only have a special (bonding) function with regard to one another as well as the consonants, but like the latter, are themselves constituents of the words whose formation they render possible.

In the light of this we need not be surprised that Plato includes motion and rest among the kinds which he wishes to investigate in order to dismantle the Eleatic canon. They certainly have lesser status than the triad being, sameness and difference, and in fact they will eventually be left behind. But they are still "very great", in so far as whichever specific thing participates in being, also participates in motion or rest. Besides, in considering the relation between being, motion and rest (in §§ 11, 12) we have prepared the ground for, and led up to, the arguments that are now to follow. Nor should it be overlooked that motion and rest are highly relevant to the is/is-not dichotomy as conceived by Parmenides. But perhaps the strongest reason for their inclusion is that Plato will need not only compatibles – and there is a sense in which sameness and difference are compatible, i.e. capable of communion – he will need incompatibles as well, and for that motion and rest have been his only candidates.

On the other hand, we may wonder why certain more deserving claimants to the title of *megista gene*, since more purely formal, have been omitted. In particular we should have expected to find unity and wholeness among the very great kinds, since a similar rank seemed to be accorded to them earlier on in the dialogue (p. 28 above). It will become obvious, however, that the five which the Stranger has chosen will be sufficient to achieve his aim. Moreover, if he had included unity, he would also have had to introduce plurality, for in so far as forms must henceforth be conceived as "wholes of parts" (p. 29 above), they obviously had to partake of plurality as well. But plurality in its own nature is indefinite, an *apeiron*, and intrinsically formless. It would appear that at the time of writing the *Sophist* Plato had not reached the point of formalizing its essence. He came close to it with the "more and less" in the *Philebus* (24 A ff.), and finally seems to have solved the problem in his unwritten doctrines with the notion of the "indeterminate dyad." There he recognized unity and plurality (thus conceived) as ultimate ontological principles, holding a place analogous to that of being, sameness and difference in our dialogue.

§ 15. The very great Kinds – Part 1: 254D–255E

The Stranger begins his survey of the five kinds with being, motion and rest whose interrelations have already been established. At 250 B–C (p. 41 f. above) he had argued that being cannot be equated with either motion or rest, nor with motion and rest together, but is a third thing. At 254 D7–12 he reaches the conclusion that each of the three is a distinct kind since two (motion and rest) cannot mingle with one another, while being mingles with both, for both motion and rest are. The incompatibility of motion and rest – "cannot mingle with one another" – is here reaffirmed. At this point the Stranger seems to accord equal status to the three kinds. He now continues:

And each of them is other than the remaining two but the same as itself (254 D14–15).[1]

There is, as Cornford saw, an implicit distinction between incompatibility and otherness (difference); for motion and rest, though other than being, combine with being, but are other than (different from), as well as incompatible with, one another.

Plato next wishes to establish that the same (sameness) and the other (difference) are two further kinds. The Stranger begins by asking what we mean by the words "the same" and "the other" (254 E2 f.), and then considers two alternatives: (i) Are they other than the three kinds already set apart but always of necessity mingled with them, or (ii) are we, in uttering them, unconsciously using a name which belongs to one or another of the three former kinds (254 E5–255 A2)? We may

---

[1] Attention is again drawn to the ambiguity of the Greek terms, rendered as "same" and "other" (cp. p. 27 n. 5):

tauton: the same, that which is the same, sameness;

thateron: the other, that which is other (different), otherness (difference).

Plato shows himself aware of these ambiguities (256A11 f., p. 74 f. below), yet does not always tell us, in which sense he uses the term.

notice that only two alternatives are considered, necessary connection or outright identity. If the last alternative is to be taken seriously, it will be pretty obvious that Plato does not regard actual linguistic usage as an unquestioned guide to ontological truth; as suggested earlier, he will accept it as a negative criterion.

Concentrating on the second alternative, the Stranger reviews in three distinct arguments the following possibilities: (a) motion and rest are [the same as] sameness or difference (255 A4–B7); (b) being and sameness are a single kind (255 B8–C7); (c) being and difference are a single kind (255 C8–E2).

(a) The first possibility is dealt with in a compact argument which by a slight rearrangement can be set out in a number of separate steps:

(i) Both motion and rest partake of sameness as well as difference (cp. 254 D14–15, p. 58 above).
(ii) But motion cannot be sameness itself, for rest combines with sameness, so that
(iii) in that case motion were to combine with rest.
(iv) And that it cannot do, for it is impossible for motion to be at rest.
(v) Nor can rest be sameness itself for corresponding reasons.
(vi) *Mutatis mutandis* neither motion nor rest can be difference itself.
(vii) Whatever we apply to motion and rest in common, such as sameness and difference, cannot be either of those two.

Since the second alternative fails, the first must hold: sameness and difference are each distinct from motion and rest, but necessarily connected with them. Once again, the nerve of the argument is the incompatibility of motion and rest, and in fact the argument here is similar to the earlier one at 252 D (p. 49 f.),[2] where the Stranger, on the strength of the incompatibility of motion and rest, established that some forms do not combine with one another, a position which is basic to the whole *megista gene* section. Significantly he now adds the further point that in the supposed case of a combination of motion with rest (and rest with motion)

whichever of the two becomes the other would force the other to change its nature into that of its opposite, since it would participate in its opposite (255 A11–B1).

Participation is here not qualified by "completely" (*pantapasi*) as at 252 D6. "Becoming the other" takes its place. Again there is no loophole for "partial participation," such as might not affect their natures (see p. 50 f. above). Still, the crucial phrase "whichever of the two

---

[2] Thus here too, as in the previous passage, we find self-predication implied (iv).

becomes the other" (255 A11) seems to cause a difficulty because any-thing, by participating in anything else, does thereby not normally become that in which it participates. Motion by participating in being does not become being, so why should motion by participating in rest become rest? Cornford tried to evade the apparent difficulty by render-ing 255 A11 "whichever of the two (motion or rest) becomes applicable to both (by being identified with either sameness or difference, which *are* applicable to both)." But "applicable," as Moravcsic (1962) p. 46 n. 1, pointed out is not warranted by the text. He offered his own so-lution to the supposed difficulty, on which, however, see F. R. Berger (1965) and Malcolm (1967) pp. 141 ff. n. 23. I submit that there is no difficulty if the incompatibility of motion and rest is taken into account. For surely, the point of the argument is that motion and rest would lose their respective identities by participating in their opposite; they would cease to be the same as themselves. There are no intermediate positions between diametrically opposed terms such as motion and rest, which together exhaust their field of applicability, just as there are none between odd and even. Consequently there are only three alternatives: either motion becomes rest, or rest becomes motion, or there is no participation. And the latter is Plato's answer: motion and rest cannot combine. Perhaps we can now accept the phrases "motion would be at rest" and "rest would be in motion" (255 A10) as a persua-sive way of stating the contradiction which would be involved if motion and rest were to partake of one another.

(b) Having shown that sameness and difference are distinct kinds from motion and rest, the Stranger now establishes that being and sameness cannot be a single kind either.

If being and sameness were not different in meaning, once more, when we say that motion and rest both are, we shall thereby be saying that both are the same (i.e. sameness, *tauton*) (255 B11–C1).

And that motion and rest cannot be sameness has already been shown. Hence sameness must be a fourth distinct kind, necessarily connected with being, as with motion and rest.

(c) The Stranger next questions whether being and difference may have to be looked upon as but two names of a single thing.[3] The pre-ceding arguments by which he has shown that sameness and being cannot be the same thing, *mutatis mutandis* could have easily been

[3] We are reminded of Plato's earlier criticisms of Parmenides whom he accused of having given two names to his one thing.

applied to the present case. The Stranger, however, uses a separate argument to prove difference a fifth kind, which he introduces by way of a distinction between two types of terms, *auta kath hauta* (in themselves) and *pros alla* (in relation to others), customarily rendered as "absolute" and "relative". I shall sometimes speak of the former as "self-contained" or "complete", of the latter as "other-relating" or "other-referring".

The distinction was much discussed at the Academy and is met with in earlier dialogues. In *Republ.* 438 A ff. Socrates gives examples of the latter type: "the greater which is such as to be greater *than* something," and similarly other comparatives, further, "the double," "the half" etc. But he also includes polar terms, such as "hot" and "cold" which are opposed to one another, next thirst which is *for* something, and knowledge which is *of* something. A good example is found in the *Phaedo* where it is said that Socrates (who is shorter than Simmias) possesses the attribute of shortness in relation to Simmias' height (102 C). Plato had no conception of relations as falling between relata; they are correlative attributes of relata. But the examples show that not only terms that establish relations between things, but any term requiring, or capable of completion and specification is considered as other-referring. The names of *infimae species* and terms descriptive of the states of a thing (e.g. sitting) would be examples of self-contained terms.

We will now set out the argument in full:

A ... of the things that are (*ton onton*), some things are always said [predicated] *auta kath hauta*, some (always) *pros alla* (255 C12 f.).
B And the different (*heteron*) is always (said [predicated]) in relation to something other (255 D1).
C It would not be so if being and difference were not very different things. If difference partook of both forms [i.e. "the in itself" (*to kath hauto*) and "other-relatedness" (*to pros allo*)] as being does, we should sometimes find among the things that are different, something that was different not in relation to another thing (255 D3–6).
D But in fact, we undoubtedly find that whatever is different is the very thing that it is [viz. different] necessarily in relation to another (255 D6 f.).
E And moreover we shall say that this nature (i.e. difference) pervades all the forms; for every one is different from the rest, not by virtue of its own nature, but because it partakes of the form (*idea*) of difference (255 E3–6).

A, on the face of it, does no more than introduce the distinction between the two kinds of terms, for the purpose of demonstrating the distinctness of being and difference (in C). I have taken "the things that are" (*ton onton*) as referring to subjects (e.g. Socrates) and "things said" to attributions of the two types in question (e.g. man, smaller).[4] Although the *kath hauto/pros allo* distinction is phrased in such a way as to make it dichotomous and exclusive, there is no reason why a "being" may not partake of both self-contained and other-referring attributes (e.g. Socrates is a man, and is smaller than Simmias). Moreover, in accordance with the two types of attribution, a subject can itself be viewed either as self-contained or other-related, since partaking mediately of these two characters (e.g. Socrates in virtue of being smaller than Simmias is related to him in a certain respect, viz. height).

B. This sentence still depends on "are said" (or "are spoken of") in A. It straightforwardly applies the distinction made there to the key term which is at issue, difference, recognising it as one of the *pros alla* class. Consequently I have rendered *to heteron* as "the different" (i.e., as naming an attribute). B would still hold if *to heteron* were rendered as "what is different" or "difference" (the form of d.), but these significations are only introduced in C, for which the ground has now been prepared.

C. "Different", then, is an attribute which things possess towards other things, and from this it follows that any statement of the form "x is different" is incomplete, until we have answered the question *pros ti*, in relation to what? C implies that things are different in virtue of their participation in the form of difference. We are led back to the meta-level, and accordingly *auto kath hauto* and *pros allo* are now spoken of as forms. Difference in its own nature is other-referring, it always partakes of "other-relatedness", but does not partake of the "in itself." It is now contrasted with being, which partakes of both forms. Hence for the reasons spelled out in C and D we cannot substitute being for difference, and the desired conclusion is drawn that difference is a fifth among the forms that have been singled out (255 D9 f.). It is distinct from, but connected with being, motion and rest, and this involves a twofold necessity: being, motion and rest necessarily participate in difference (see p. 59), and that participation is necessarily other-referring (D).

It is worth noting that by the same criterion by which difference has been distinguished from being, any *pros allo* form could be distinguished

4 Another reading is however possible. Since *kath hauto* and *pros allo* terms do not only function as attributes, but some of them as subjects as well, we may take "the things that are" (*ton onton*) as referring to the two types of terms, which gives us the following version of A: "Of the things that are some are always spoken of as *auta kath hauta*, some as *pros alla*."

from being. Difference, though, is in a privileged position, since it is all-pervading like being and co-extensive with it. Whatever participates in being, participates in difference as well. (E).

The most significant and intriguing feature is the participation of being in both "the in-itself" and "other-relatedness". It will be discussed in the next section.[5]

---

[5] Some writers have seen reason to expand A in the light of C and D, e.g. Cornford (1935), see p. 281 n. 1, and especially Frede (1967). I feel, however, that A does no more than straightforwardly introduce the *kath hauto/pros allo* distinction, and that building up from there A–D offers a sustained and conclusive argument.

§ 16. Comment on Part I

1. In discussing these passages, we may wonder why Plato went to such length to establish the distinct existence of his five chosen kinds. Who might ever wish to confound difference or sameness with motion or rest, or any of those four with being? For us at least these are distinct notions, and on the face of it, Plato's exercise has a somewhat quixotic look. We may find good reasons for it, however, if we remember that being, difference and sameness, and (motion + rest) are co-extensive. Moreover these notions tended to be conglomerated in the doctrines of his predecessors, and even in his own earlier thinking. With his emancipation from the Eleatic heritage, Plato had reached a new vantage point from which Heraclitus, for instance, might appear to have confused being with motion (flux), while it could be said of Parmenides that he had rolled being, sameness and rest into one solid ball.[1] And was not Plato's own "classical" form a conglomerate of the very same ingredients? Plato must have felt a need to differentiate these various strands as he undertook to weave them into a new fabric.

2. The Stranger has not discussed the possibility that difference and sameness might perhaps be two names of a single thing (the question which he raised about difference and the other three kinds).[2] The reason is, not that he considered them as most opposed to one another, but that he recognized sameness only in relation to self (i.e. he only recognized what we should call self-identity) and difference only in relation to other. Thus sameness and difference are two sides of one coin, as it were – complementary notions, and difference from other and sameness with self are mutually implicative. They combine with each other. Yet they are distinct and irreducible kinds. Hence "different from other"

---

[1] The "sphere"; see p. 27 above.
[2] Although he refers to such Sophistic arguments as "the same is different or the different is the same," etc. (259 D).

is not equivalent with "not the same as the other," nor is "the same as itself" equivalent with "not different from itself." Same does not apply to other, nor different to self. Consequently Plato does not use locutions corresponding to "is the same as," "is not the same as" when the entities in question are designated by different names. He asks whether sameness and difference are other (*allo* 254 E3) than being, motion and rest, or whether we are unconsciously using a name that belongs to one or another of those three kinds (255 A1 f.). He argues that neither rest nor motion can *be* anything that we say of both in common (255 A7 f.), and concludes that we must not say that sameness or difference *are* motion or rest (255 B5 f., cp. A4 f.). Again, he speaks of difference in meaning (255 B11), he says that sameness and being cannot be one thing (255 C3), and he questions whether difference and being must be thought of as two names for a single kind (255 C9 f.). We can, of course, meaningfully expand "be" (at 255 A7), and "are" (at 255 B5 and A4) into "be the same as" and "are the same as" respectively, and similarly in other places, and conclude that the verb "to be" is here used as identity-sign, to express negative identity between motion and rest on the one hand, and sameness and difference on the other. But if so, we should miss, I believe, Plato's intention. For when we think in terms of negative identity, Plato thinks in terms of participation in difference, where difference is a positive predicate. Differentiation into kinds is a positive feature of reality. This I take to be the message of the concluding sentence (E, p. 61 above). And when Plato says that difference cannot be located in the peculiar nature of any individual form, he establishes difference as a meta-formal character. There is also an unmistakable pointer to its vowel function, in so far as it is said to pervade all forms, for this involves separating them kind by kind, and so making it possible for the dialectician to undertake his divisions (cp. p. 53 above).[3] Lastly, there is an implied distinction between difference and incompatibility. Forms are different from one another, not in virtue of their own natures but because they participate in the form of difference.[4] It is in virtue of their own natures, however, as we have seen, that some forms cannot combine, i.e. are incompatible with one another.

---

[3] The vowel function of the likewise all-pervasive form of sameness is collateral, in so far as it provides for the self-identity of each form as the latter is traversed, and mingles with others.

[4] Of course, participation in difference implies that the forms concerned have each a specific nature of their own.

3. Why has the Stranger used a separate argument to establish difference as a fifth kind distinct from being, and did not avail himself of the argument by simple substitution which had served him in the case of sameness and being? There are a number of answers:

Difference calls for special treatment because for once it is far more important than its collateral, sameness. Sameness figures prominently in the doctrine of isolated Parmenidoid forms; the science of dialectic and method of division hinges on difference. Moreover, Plato will presently show that the different is the true nature of not-being so that "is not" can in all cases be understood as "is different from . . . ," i.e. as "participates in difference in relation to . . .". Difference in relation to other (*pros allo*) will be pivotal in defeating the Eleatic canon, and this is a strong reason for introducing other-relatedness when establishing difference as a distinct kind.

But there is still more to the Stranger's procedure. We may remember that it is our goal to understand being as well as not-being. Having been unable to define being, we are still in the dark about both, but believe that the understanding of one may also shed light on the other (p. 43). In the pair *to pros allo* and *to kath hauto* Plato has found an intrinsic meta-formal characterization, by reference to which being and difference (and therefore not-being) can be distinguished from one another, and thereby illumine one another.

4. The *to pros allo/to kath hauto* distinction is thus of relevance to our goal. When the Stranger tells us that being partakes of both, he refers to the "in itself" and "other relatedness" as forms. Why forms? Why is he not satisfied with his introductory statement that of the things that are (*ton onton*) some things are always said as in themselves, some as in relation to others (255 C12 f., p. 61)? [5] He appears to hold that *onta*, either mediately or immediately (according to the reading of A which we adopt), can only be spoken of as *auta kath hauta* and *pros alla*, because the form of being (*on*) participates in the forms of *to kath hauto* and *to pros allo*. For Plato modes of language reflect, and direct attention to, ontological relations on which they depend, a point which we already noted in connection with his arguments for the combination of forms and the possibility of synthetic statements (pp. 49 ff.). And did he not, on that very occasion, argue that unless forms combined, we could not speak of anything as, among other things, *kath hauto* (252 C4)?

---

[5] Or on the other suggested reading (p. 62 n. 4) that of the things that are some are always spoken of etc.

In this sense, the combination of being with the two forms is a necessary condition for anything to be spoken of in these ways.[6]

But the more important question is, what does the Stranger tell us about the form of being, when he says that it partakes of both the "in itself" and "other-relatedness"? Clearly, only forms referred to by relative (incomplete) terms partake, and all such forms must partake, of the *pros allo*; otherwise forms are *auta kath hauta*. Being, too, will be *auto kath hauto*, and this causes as little difficulty as the *pros allo* character of difference. But in which sense can being partake of *to pros allo*, that is, can being, too, be incomplete and therefore be an incomplete determination of the forms that partake of it?

In answering this question we must once again take into account that not-being is to be interpreted in terms of its true nature, difference, and remember that we expect our understanding of being and not-being will grow *pari passu*.

Now not-being (like difference) is not *auto kath hauto*, it does not partake of the "in itself," it is always in relation to something other. From this it follows that to say "x is not" is to utter an incomplete sentence in the same way as if one were to say "x is different" without indicating what it was different from. To make a complete statement, we have to say "x is not y," which in turn can be analysed into "x is different from (= x participates in difference in relation to) y."

Being, on the other hand, is *auto kath hauto*, it does partake of the "in itself". Hence "x is" is a complete sentence, and accordingly Plato will say "Motion is", "Motion and rest are" (e.g. 250 A11, 254 D10, 256 A1) etc., and indicate that this is so because they combine with or participate in being. So far there is no sense of being *pros allo* involved. Nor do we require that sense to establish that whatever participates in being must have a nature of its own. For that has always been Plato's view. As Stenzel pointed out, Plato only knows being as filled with intuitional content ("anschaulichem Inhalt," 1961 p. 96, Engl. ed. 136 f.), and that content is intuitively apprehended as what it is (e.g. the beautiful). But the other-relatedness of being is required at the stage

---

[6] Frede (1967) p. 24 complains that Cornford, Moravcsic, Runciman and others have treated *auta kath hauta* and *pros alla* as properties of things and even assumed forms for them. But compare the phrase *amphoin meteiche toin eidoin* (participated in those two forms) at 255 D4. Frede points out that they are modes or ways in which a predicate is affirmed of an object. This is certainly the case. But it does seem to be Plato's view that we can only speak of things in those ways, because of the underlying ontological relation. This is brought out here as much as in the earlier passage referred to above. The combination of forms is Plato's answer to Eleaticism and its Sophistic derivates, and the struggle with them is present to his mind throughout the *megista gene* sections.

of Plato's thinking at which he realized that dialectic is built on a combination of *eide*. At this point statements of the form "x is" can in an important sense be seen to be incomplete. The forms at large are elucidated in terms of other forms, i.e. other natures in which they participate, or of others again, in relation to which they participate in difference. To participate in being implies to participate in a good many other things, to *be* means to be related to those other things. In this sense, being is intrinsically other-relating. The Stranger will later put it thus:

So in the case of every one of the forms being (*to on*) is (*esti*) many, and not-being [i.e. that which is different from it] is infinite in number (256 E5 f., p. 76 below).

Being (like difference) is an all-pervasive meta-form, fulfilling its vowel function in virtue of its other-relatedness. The important upshot of the position now reached is, that although being – like the other meta-forms – is non-descriptive, the natures that participate in being, in virtue of that participation, are capable of being described.

In affirming other-relatedness of being as well as not-being, Plato illumines the nature of both. "To be" means to be something specific, and related, and thus capable of being described. "To be-not" does not mean to be nothing at all (*to medamos on*, § 4). It means to be not something else, and therefore to be different from it. This implies that both that which is different, and that from which it is different have being and possess each their own specific natures (cp. p. 65 n. 4). All the terms involved are namable and describable. It is in this way that Plato fills Parmenides' empty notion of "it is," [7] and overcomes the logically vitiating sense of "it is not" which the latter had bequeathed to philosophy, and which had ended up as the Sophist's hiding-place.

5. To those acquainted with recent literature on the *Sophist* it may come as a surprise that nothing has been said on these pages concerning the various senses of the verb "to be", i.e. the existential, identity and predicative or attributive (copular) senses which we have learned to distinguish. It has been the view of Ackrill, Moravcsic, and to some extent Runciman that one, perhaps the most important aspect of the *megista gene* sections is the clarification of these senses which, they hold, had been confused, and could therefore give rise to such puzzles as that of the "late learners". There is no evidence, though, in the dialogue that Plato concerned himself with the ambiguities of the verb

---

[7] Parmenides had himself tried to fill his empty *estin* (it is) by a number of attributions to which, however, according to Plato's earlier arguments, he was not entitled (§ 8 above).

"to be" (*einai*).[8] Nor does the game of the "late learners", in treating every subject as a miniature edition of Eleatic being, rest on a confusion between two senses of the verb "to be", viz. identity and attribution. Their position (though they may not have been all that serious about it) implies that an attributive sense is logically impossible. Plato did distinguish between the intension and the extension of "being". And he was obviously faced with the Eleatic notion of empty being, which we may designate as a pure existential sense.[9] But Plato never accepted that sense. For him participation in being implies what we may call "being as". When he says "motion is" or "motion and rest are," he does not use the verb "to be" in our "existential" sense.[10] Motion *is* as moving, and only as moving, it *is* as a "what," a "nature." And Plato seems willing to pay the unavoidable price of self-predication for this position (cp. pp. 42 n. 2, 49.). Regarding an identity sense of "to be" that can be discerned in such sentences as "motion is not the same," which Plato takes to be sanctioned by the participation of motion in difference towards sameness, I refer to previous remarks (p. 64 f.). Surely when Plato interprets "is not" in terms of "participates in difference in relation to ..." he is not intent on clarifying an identity sense of the verb "to be." Nor are the "late learners" his target. His concern, as throughout these sections, is the dismantling of the Eleatic canon. He wants to show that what is-not, in some respects is – an aim altogether different from establishing negative identity.

The question which interests us in the context of the present section is whether "being in relation to other" can be interpreted in terms of the function of the copular "is" in statements. Among the writers

[8] The most thorough treatment of the question is by Frede (1967) who concluded that Plato did not distinguish an existential from a copulative "is"; compare Owen (1970) p. 257 f. Frede himself, however, discovered two usages of "is" in the *Sophist* in accordance with *kath hauto* and *pros allo* predications.

[9] It is "pure" because it does not allow for descriptive fillings. Not without justification did Taran (1965) render Parmenides' *estin* (it is) as "exists"; cp. Guthrie (1965) p. 28.

I cannot agree with Kahn (1966) that Parmenides' doctrine of Being is first and foremost a doctrine concerning reality as *what is the case* (p. 251). Kahn is surely right that what is the case (*Sachverhalte*) is a primary sense of the Greek verb "to be." But Parmenides did not allow for anything to be the case except being *qua se*. He divested that sense of its content, and it was one of Plato's tasks to restore it.

Nor can I concur with Mourelatos (1970) in interpreting Parmenides' subjectless *estin* as the "is" of speculative predication. Parmenides' is not a doctrine of method that can be applied but a doctrine of being. This was certainly Plato's understanding of it, whatever his distortions (p. 25 above). Consequently I follow Guthrie (1965) in supplying *to eon* as the implied subject which, however, I would wish to render not as "what is" but as "Being." Although Parmenides could not but express himself in the spatial mode, his concern was the meaning of being – not the universe.

[10] So also Owen (1970) *passim*.

mentioned, Moravcsic put forward the view that *einai pros allo*, which he called "relational being", shows that Plato recognized "the connection between subject and predicate as an aspect of the form of being" (1962, p. 54 f.). On this view being *pros allo* would become the "form of predication." But Plato does not require a form of predication. Although Plato uses the copular "is", he accounts for the connection between the entities to which subject and predicate refer, in terms of an ontological relation which he expresses as combination, participation, etc., words which do not stand for forms. They are topic-neutral operators, which are not designated *within* his ontology. The very great kinds, and being and difference in particular, make combinations (which include separations) *possible*. But at the same time they are themselves ontological constituents which enter into combinations (see p. 57), and therefore cannot function as combining operators. Moravcsic, however, and similarly Runciman, would require us to re-translate "participation" into "being *pros allo*." If this was Plato's version of the copular "is", we should be faced with the further difficulty that "being *pros allo*" is itself complex, and on Plato's philosophical analysis must be rendered as "being participates in other relatedness towards...". It would therefore appear that the suggested translation of "participation" into "being *pros allo*" implies a second participation, and to be consistent, that, once again, would require to be accounted for in terms of being *pros allo*. But this would not only engender an infinite regress but give us a copula within the copula which is absurd. I conclude that being *pros allo* cannot be identified as copula.

Moreover, we can only reduce a complex ontological relation to a "syntactical sign," which is Kahn's (1966) designation of the copula, at the price of ignoring Plato's view that the expressions we use are logically dependent upon the structure of reality (cp. pp. 46, 66 f.). It is because being participates (operator!) in other relatedness (vowel function!) that the forms at large, *qua* participating in being, participate in one another, and we are enabled to make valid participation statements about them which we may cast into copular form, if we wish.[11]

6. There remain a number of points concerning the "in itself" and "other – relatedness", in particular with reference to difference and sameness.

[11] It seems characteristic of the direction of Plato's thinking that in the examples of the interrelations of the great kinds, which he will offer (§ 17), a participation statement is given as the ground of (and in most cases precedes) the statement of the same relation in "is" or "is not" form.

(a) We may wonder whether all forms *qua* forms, regardless whether they function as complete or other-referring predicates, must not be what they are, just in themselves, must not be *auta kath hauta*. This question raises difficulties concerning difference which was said to be always *pros allo*. For to meet the point, difference would have to participate in both *to kath hauto* and *to pros allo*, like being.[12] But if so, Plato's argument for the distinctness of difference as a separate kind would collapse. The problem is analogous to the one we raised with regard to the form of motion (p. 51), when we asked whether motion, *qua* form and *qua* knowable, must not be at rest. To meet these dilemmas Plato would have had to distinguish between the form as a definite nature, and the form *qua* form, and between the attributes that appertain to it when considered in the latter sense, from the one belonging to it in the former. Plato certainly moved towards such a distinction with the introduction of his "meta-forms", being, difference and sameness, in which all forms participate, and in virtue of which they *are*, are differentiated and self-identical. But the meta-line was never too sharply drawn, and I doubt whether in his own thinking he separated his form conception from the forms of which he conceived. The forms were natures, ontological constituents and even the *megista gene* – those "superlative things" – were thought of in this way. Thus it was of the nature of difference to be always *pros allo*. Take the nature away, and what is left? If the *eide* and *gene* of the *Sophist* had been concepts (§ 1, p. 2), the abstraction required to meet the case would have caused no problem. In fact, that there is this difficulty, which Plato cannot resolve, may be added evidence that we are not entitled to assess forms as concepts, even in the *Sophist*. (cp. also § 18 below.)

(b) A problem may be thought to arise concerning sameness. Surely this form is *auto kath hauto* if anything is, for the only sameness that Plato knows is self-sameness. Consequently, if we say of anything that it partakes of sameness, we affirm that it is complete in itself, and no relation to others is involved. Indeed, no form is ever "the same" as any other, each is its own individual self. If we ask, however, how Plato expresses self-sameness, the answer will be: motion (*kinesis*) participates in sameness towards itself (*pros heauten*) (256 B1). True, sameness is not *pros allo*, but it still is *pros ti*, related to something. Yet although participation in sameness is always towards self, its

---

[12] There will in fact be two places where the context requires us to understand "difference" *auto kath hauto* (pp. 75, 85 f. n. 2 below).

affirmation is not an analytic proposition. Sameness is a distinct kind, and to say that motion participates in sameness (towards self), is not equivalent to saying motion is motion. It is not a tautology but what we call a synthetic *a priori* proposition. And the same applies *mutatis mutandis* to the affirmations concerning the other kinds. This feature, I think lends support to my view that we are here concerned with ontological relations rather than with conceptual analyses.

The Stranger will now finally settle with Parmenides and establish that what is-not in some respect *is*, and that what is, in a way is-not (cp. 241 D5–7, p. 21 above). In making good his challenge he will also hit the Sophist and his band of pseudo-Eleatics, "late learners" and contradiction mongers. Being and not-being do combine, "is" and "is-not" statements are compatible, in fact imply one another, and their contradiction is merely apparent.

His procedure will be as follows: He begins with one of his very great kinds and examines its possible relations with the remaining four. Taking motion, he will indicate eight such relations, and these can conveniently be arranged in four pairs. As he states each pair, he shows how it can be recast in "is" – "(is) not" form, thereby generating contradictions (except in the case of the first pair). But these contradictions are only apparent, i.e. we "escape unscathed," because the ontological account from which they have been distilled is free from contradiction. Rather than analysing given contradictions, the Stranger shows how apparent contradictions may arise through failure to take into account the precise sense and respect in which the great kinds apply (259 D1–2). In producing them, he certainly shows himself a master of the art of sophistry, but it is only by ignoring the ontology which underlies the apparent contradictions, that interpreters may have been led to regard his arguments as sophistic (e.g. Peck, 1952).

As is often the case, Plato introduces his subject in a casual manner, and the first pair looks pretty innocuous:

1st pair
{
(1) Motion is altogether (*pantapasin*) different from [i.e. participates in difference in relation to] rest (255 E11 f.).
(2) Motion participates in being (256 A1).
}

The term *pantapasin* we met before in connection with motion and rest (252 D6), when we discussed the impossibility of their mutual participation (cp. pp. 49 ff.). Here Plato may use the term in order to convey once again that there is more than difference, namely incompatibility, that holds them apart. The recast version of the first pair is as follows:

1st pair $\begin{cases} (1') \text{ Motion is not rest (255 E14).}^1 \\ (2') \text{ Motion is (256 A1).} \end{cases}$

There is no obvious contradiction between these two statements, although a Parmenidean neophyte might read one into them, by contending that any "is-not" statement implies the not-being of its subject. But not much turns on the first pair. The next two pairs can be taken in conjunction:

2nd pair $\begin{cases} (3) \text{ Motion is different from [i.e. participates in difference in relation} \\ \quad \text{to] the same (sameness) (256 A3).} \\ (4) \text{ Motion participates in the same (sameness) in relation to itself} \\ \quad (256 \text{ A7 f. cp. B1).} \end{cases}$

3rd pair $\begin{cases} (5) \text{ Motion is different from [i.e. participates in difference in relation} \\ \quad \text{to] difference (itself) (256 C5 f.).} \\ (6) \text{ Motion participates in difference in relation to x y z. [(6) is not} \\ \quad \text{spelled out in the text].} \end{cases}$

The two pairs are recast as follows:

2nd pair (3'–4') Motion is both the same and not the same (sameness) (256 A10).

3rd pair (5'–6') Motion in a sense is not (the) different (difference) and also different (256 C8).

The Stranger supplies a careful elucidation of (3'–4'), and this *mutatis mutandis* applies equally to (5'–6'). Here is what he says:

(A10) Motion, then is (*einai*) both the same and not the same: we must admit that without being disturbed by it. – (A11) For when we call it the same and not the same, we do not speak alike [do not use the word in the same sense]: we call it the same because of its participation in "the same" (sameness) in relation to itself, and not "the same" (sameness) on account of its combination with difference, by which it is separated off from "the same" (sameness), and becomes not that but different, and is in turn correctly spoken of as "not the same." (256 A10–B4).

Here the appearance of contradiction is created by the ambiguity of the Greek term *tauton* (and in (5'–6') of *heteron*) which may mean "same" as well as "the same" or "sameness" (and respectively "different" as well as "the different" or "difference"). The ambiguity is thus

---

[1] Comparing (1') with (1) we may realize that it would be wrong to expand "... is not rest" into "... is not the same as rest"; see previous argument on "negative identity," pp. 64 f. and 68 f. above.

due to the double usage of these words as adjectives and neuter nouns (cp. pp. 27, n. 5, 58 n. 1 above). In the quoted passage Plato shows himself aware of the ambiguity.[2]

Concerning (5) we may notice that the form of difference from which motion is different, must be taken as *auto kath hauto* (cp. p. 71 above), otherwise (5) would be synonymous with (6). Cornford's interpretation (1935) p. 287 does in fact make (5) and (6) synonymous, and thereby blurs the intended contradiction in the derived statement (5′–6′).

To avoid the *kath hauto/pros allo* dilemma concerning (5) Plato might have been better off if he had been able to render "is different from difference" as "is not the same as difference." But this he could not do, since he only recognized sameness in relation to self. Difference, as pointed out before, is a positive character that does not do duty for a denial of sameness; it is complementary to it, and this is the reason why sameness and difference can combine with one another.

We come now to the last and crucial pair:

4th pair
{
(7) Motion is different from [i.e. participates in difference in relation to] being (256 D5).
(8) Motion participates in being (256 D9).
}

Since motion participates in being, it *is*, and since it is different (separated) from being, it is-not. Hence we can make bold and say

4th pair (7′–8′) Motion really is a thing that is-not and a thing that is (256 D8 f.).

We may note that proposition (8) is identical with proposition (2) in our first pair, but while the contradiction which can be imported into (1′–2′) is a Sophistic development of Eleatic doctrine, (7′–8′) outright dismantles the Eleatic canon: for on the Stranger's ontological analysis the "is-not" in (7′–8′) does not entail a denial of being, but amounts to an affirmation of difference from the form of being. Thus he has succeeded in showing, as he set out to show, that what is-not in a sense

---

[2] Runciman (1962) p. 89, following Ackrill (1957), argues to the effect that Plato is not distinguishing between senses of *tauton* but between two different senses of *einai*. Motion both is (copula) the same as itself and is not (identity sign) sameness. The passage is phrased in such a way, however, as to make this interpretation unlikely. Plato does not at A 10 formulate the contradiction as R. suggests: "motion is the same and is not the same"; but says: "motion is the same and not the same," using the verb "to be" (*einai*) only once. Moreover, in the second sentence, beginning at A11, where Plato deals with the ambiguity, he does not mention the verb "to be" at all, but repeats "the same" and "not the same," and this strongly suggests that it is the word "same" of which we are "not speaking alike." Moreover, if I am right that Plato did not have a notion of negative identity it would seem implausible that he singled out "is-not" as identity sign, the less so, since he had quite different aims for its interpretation (cp. pp. 64 f. and 68 f. above). Compare Owen (1970) p. 258 n. 63.

is, and in which sense it is. He will in due course show the sense in which what is, in a way is-not.

It may by now have become clear why the Stranger had to recast the eight relations, in which each of the great kinds stands to the other four, and thereby generate contradictions, such as had been outlawed by Father Parmenides. The purpose of the exercise is not to single out the copular and identity senses of the verb "to be," which *we* can discern in the derived statements, but to present a series of combinations of being and not-being which culminate in the challenging assertion that motion both is and is-not.

Plato's key move is his discovery that the true nature of not-being is "difference". This enables him to interpret even a simple denial such as "x is-not," whatever x may stand for, as an affirmation of difference, in this case from the form of being. Parmenides should not have said "Is *or* is-not" but "Participates in *and* is different from" which may be recast as a paradoxical "Is *and* is-not." The Eleatic disjunction has been replaced by a conjunction, tautology by synthetic *a priori* truth. This is a brilliant philosophical transformation, but unfortunately Plato has overshot his mark, for he has not left himself any elbow room for a legitimate denial of the existence of anything whatsoever.[3] This, though, might not have troubled him in the present context, since he is here only concerned with forms.

The Stranger now extends the conclusion reached in (7'–8') regarding motion to all forms. They participate in being and in difference in relation to the form of being, and therefore we are justified in saying that they both are and are-not (256 D11–E3). The Stranger continues:

So in the case of every one of the forms, being (*to on*) is (*esti*) many, and not-being [i.e. that which is different from it] is infinite in number (256 E5 f.).[4]

This affirmation depends on the other-relatedness of being and not-being as an additional premise (cp. p. 68 above). It refers to all the other forms in which every one of the forms participates in virtue of its participation in being, as well as those in relation to which it participates in difference in virtue of its participation in not-being. Naturally

---

[3] Cp. Crombie (1963), pp. 500, 510 f.

[4] Being and not-being must here be taken *in extenso*. Cornford, p. 288 does not make "being" but "every one of the forms" the subject of the main clause, rendering it "there is much that *it* is." This, while certainly true, is not what Plato literally says.

the latter are infinite in number.[5] But what is true of all forms must be true of the form of being itself: it, too, must be called different from all the others (257 A1 f.), a conclusion which is recast as follows:

> We find, then, that being likewise is-not in as many respects as there are other things; for not being those others, while it is its single self, it is-not that indefinite number of other things (257 A4–6).

This gives us the sense in which being itself is-not and so makes good the second half of the challenge to Parmenides.

While the Stranger says "being is-not", he will not, as in the case of motion and of the forms generally, assert that "Being both is and is-not." Instead he pairs the not-being of being with "its single self." It is difficult to make out whether this phrase is to refer to the participation of being in sameness towards itself, or to its participation in the "in itself" or to both. I favour the first alternative because it brings out the mutual implication between sameness towards self and difference towards others (which is the implied interpretation of "not being those others"). Moreover, it entitles us to infer that being and not-being are similarly related as sameness and difference. As was shown earlier, for anything to participate in being, it must be specific, a nature of its own,[6] and being that nature (being its "single self," as we may now perhaps say), it must be different from an indefinite number of others, hence must "not-be" those others. To participate in being entails participating in not-being and *vice versa*. Being and not-being are not "most opposed to one another" but complementary notions that imply one another. Q.E.D.

---

[5] To justify that the things from which any form differs are infinite in number, it is not necessary to invoke "negative identity" as Owen (1970) p. 254 does. While any determinate nature has many, though not an infinite number of, attributes (forms in which it participates) it must be different from an infinite number of others. On "negative identity" cp. p. 64 f. above.

[6] Its participation in other forms can here be left out of consideration.

§ 18. Motion and Rest once more: 256B6–C4

In the course of the preceding argument we find the following passage which calls for separate discussion:

> Stranger   So, too, supposing that motion itself did in any way participate in rest, there would be nothing outrageous in speaking of it as stationary.
>
> Theaet.   Perfectly correct, provided that we are to agree that some of the kinds will blend with one another, and others will not.
>
> Stranger   Well, that is a conclusion we proved at an earlier stage, when we showed that such was indeed according to their nature (*kata phusin*).
>
> Theaet.   Yes, of course.

The passage comes immediately after Plato has shown in which sense it is legitimate to say that motion both is the same and not the same. It may therefore be tempting to infer that it is equally legitimate to say that motion both is at rest and not at rest. But while in the former case Plato told us in which sense motion may be said to be the same and not the same (viz. as participating in sameness towards itself and in difference towards the form of sameness) no such indication is forthcoming in the present case.

On the face of it, any suggestion of a participation of motion in rest (however cautiously worded), seems inconsistent with all previous passages in which the two forms were considered, and where any relationship between them was excluded, except their participation in difference in regard to one another. We will briefly review the arguments in question:

(a) At 250A f. (p. 41 f.) the Stranger pointed out that motion and rest are most opposed (*enantiotata*) to one another, which we may take as affirming their incompatibility. This was used as an argument to establish that being is a distinct kind from motion and rest, although both motion and rest partake of it.

(b) At 252D (p. 49 f.) the Stranger argued that motion and rest cannot combine with one another, for in that case motion itself would come to a complete standstill, and rest itself would be in movement – dismissed as absolute impossibilities. This argument was offered as the only proof for the position that not all forms are capable of combining. The aim of the whole passage was to establish that some forms will combine while others will not.

(c) At 254D the incompatibility of motion and rest was reaffirmed (p. 59), and at 255A f. the Stranger argued that sameness cannot be another name for motion and/or rest, for that would force either of these two to change its nature into that of its opposite, since it would participate in its opposite (p. 59 f.). The argument for sameness as a distinct kind thus hinged on the impossibility of a combination of motion and rest.

Cornford (1935) believed that the present passage was inconsistent with the previously established position, and to overcome the discrepancy, thought it necessary to emend the text (p. 286 f., n. 3) – a desperate move, according to one of his critics. I myself think that to make sense of the present passage, no emendation of the text is needed. On the other hand, whatever has been said concerning motion and rest there is still the problem that motion *qua* form and object of knowledge must be immovable (see p. 51). But it was not, I suggested, within Plato's conceptual reach to achieve the required separation of form *qua* form from form *qua* "nature" (p. 71). Frede (1967) p. 34, however, considers the present passage as evidence that he did perhaps make that distinction, and refers to the careful formulation ("in any way"), which indicates to him that Plato, while ascribing rest to the form of motion did not want to ascribe it to motion *qua* motion. He thinks that the discussion of that very distinction by Aristotle (*Topics* 137 b7 ff.) allows the inference that it was made at the Academy.

But of course, Plato does not make that distinction here. The participation of motion in rest is put forward as a supposal, and no reason is given for it: if motion did in any way participate in rest, then it would not be absurd to speak of it as at rest. Theaetetus assents: in that case it would indeed not be absurd, provided we agree that some forms will combine, and some will not. But that some forms will not combine was established by reference to the very impossibility of the mutual participation of motion and rest. And promptly the Stranger refers to that earlier proof.

I can think of two possible interpretations:

(a) The Stranger may wish to make the point that there are pairs of contrasted kinds, such as being and not-being, sameness and difference, which everyone regards as contraries, and whose alleged contrariety is exploited to "parade contradictions in argument," but that we have shown that they combine with one another, and that those contradictions are only apparent. There are, however, other kinds whose contrariety is real and irreducible since grounded in their nature (*kata phusin*). Thus seen, the passage represents a (perhaps timely) reminder of the importance of incompatibility, and there seems no need for us to emend the text in order to convey this message.

(b) Plato may indeed have toyed with the idea that motion itself, one of the very great kinds, needs to be immovable. This is suggested by a striking parallel with his handling of the *dunamis* criterion at 248D (pp. 34 ff.). There it was a question of whether forms are moved in being known; here it is the question of motion to be at rest in order to be known. In both cases the respective positions are put forward as a supposal. And it is my view that Plato retracts in the present case as he did in the former (cp. p. 38). The reason now is that he has not the conceptual facility of an Aristotle, let alone of twentieth century interpreters, to make the categorical distinction between formal and *kata phusin* requirements, which is needed in order to satisfy both without thereby falling into contradiction.

§ 19. The Not-Beautiful, the Not-Just and the Not-Tall: 257B–258C

The Stranger now draws out certain implications from what he has established (§ 17). Recalling his interpretation of "is-not" in terms of "is different from," he asks us to grant that we do not mean by "that which is-not" something contrary (opposed, *enantion*) to what is but something that is different [from it] (257 B3 f.). From this it only takes a short step to the general axiom

that the prefix "not" indicates something different from the words that follow it, or rather from the things designated by the words pronounced after the negative (257 B10–C3).

Let us call what is thus designated as different, the "not-x". It is at least one purpose of the present section to affirm that the not-x possesses as much being as the x (257 E9 f., 258 A1 f., 5). Plato's three examples of not-x are the not-beautiful, the not-tall and the not-just.

The Stranger makes a second approach by introducing an analogy between the nature of the different (difference) and knowledge. Just as there are many arts and kinds of knowledge, although knowledge itself is one (i.e. a single kind) so the single nature of the different has many parts (257 C–D). These "parts" of the different are the not-x's, and since the different belongs to the things that are (i.e., the form of difference partakes of being, as we have learned), so do its parts (258 A9).

What is the nature and range of the not-x's, and in which sense can they be said to be "parts" of the different (difference)? What is the value of the whole argument which does not, on the face of it, add anything to the position already reached?

The terms – the beautiful, the tall and the just – are beset by a similar ambiguity as noted regarding "the same" and "the different". They mean both "the beautiful itself" (the form of beauty) etc. and that which is beautiful, and so on. But in one place at least the Stranger identifies the beautiful as a single definite kind (257 E2). So it seems that it is forms which are meant, and not particulars. From this it is reasonable to conclude that the not-beautiful etc. also refer to forms, though particulars are not necessarily excluded. Since Plato in the not much later *Politicus* (262 C ff.) denied forms of such terms as not-Greek, not-tenthousand, it is unlikely that he considered the not-beautiful as "a single definite kind" like the beautiful, and so in the case of his other examples. He may use these negative terms collectively to refer to all those forms that are different from the beautiful, i.e., to an indefinite number of them. This would well accord with 256 E5 f. (p. 76) where he said that "in the case of every one of the forms . . . not-being [i.e. that which is different from it] is infinite in number." Now while it is true that every form is different from all the others, it seems that Plato in the present section, by designating these others as the not-beautiful, the not-tall and the not-just respectively, tells us something about the nature of the not-x's which he has in mind. He does not, as in the preceding section, affirm difference from an indefinite number *tout court*, he affirms difference from a number of forms which in some sense are relevant to the x's. Their number of course will still be indefinite, but all will belong to the same family as the x's. That this is Plato's thinking comes out in two ways:

(i) In several places Plato speaks of his not-x's as contrasted (*antithesis*) with the x's (e.g. 257 D7, E3, 6) and at 258 B1–3 *antithesis* is explicitly distinguished from *enantion*, contrary. In other words, the not-x's though different, are generically the same as the x's, they belong to the same family. Otherwise there would be no contrast.

(ii) At 257 B6 f. the Stranger mentions that when we speak of something as not-tall, we may just as well mean by that phrase what is equal [in size] as what is short. Both terms belong to the same family as the tall, for all three refer to size.[1]

In this connection a difficulty arises. The Stranger has argued that the not-x's, though contrasted with the x's, are not their contraries. But obviously short is the contrary of tall, unless it is Plato's understanding that all size terms by their very nature are *pros allo*: they certainly are in their application to particulars (cp. *Phaedo* 102 C). Still, I do not see how we can exclude what is unjust and ugly from the range of the not-just and the not-beautiful. On the other hand, Plato

---

[1] This passage seems to confirm that Plato thought of the not-x's as classes which comprise forms, e.g. the equal, the short, etc., but are not themselves forms.

might hold that we are no longer justified in speaking simply of not-x, i.e. in terms of difference from x, when the qualities referred to are *pantapasi* different. They are most opposed to the x's, and that not in virtue of their participation in difference but of their own nature. On balance, however, I have come to the conclusion that Plato did include in the not-x's qualities that are incompatible with the x's, for he will later treat of flying and sitting (which are incompatibles) in this way.[2]

In what sense can the not-x be spoken of as a "part" of difference? If we follow the thought developed in earlier sections, only in the sense that x participates in difference in relation to the indefinite number of kinds or forms which not-x denotes. Now these forms each have a nature of their own (e.g. short, equal). But it is not in virtue of the nature of the forms denoted by not-x, that not-x may be spoken of as part of difference. This needs saying because the designation "parts of difference" has been introduced by way of an analogy with kinds of knowledge, and there is the suspicion that difference is here treated as a genus and any not-x as one of its species. But the very great kinds are not genera which can be divided into species. Nor is the not-x a species of anything. It is not a form with a nature of its own, but an umbrella under which we collect an indefinite number of kindred forms in virtue of a meta-formal character which they all possess, viz. participation in difference in relation to x. The expression "part", though not a happy one, can in this manner be rendered innocuous. The very great kinds have no parts except in the extensional sense that they encompass (encircle) whatever participates in them. So far, so good.

Still, the terminology subsequently becomes equivocal so that the distinction between not-x as formally determined, and x as specifically determined is hard to maintain. The concluding argument (258 A11–C3) can by slight rearrangement be set out in four steps:

(1) The not-x *qua* part of the nature of the different is contrasted with x *qua* part of the nature of being.[3]
(2) Not-x is as much an *ousia* as being itself.
(3) Since what is different (or difference) is the nature of what is-not (or not-being), not-being is as much an *ousia* as being itself.
(4) As the tall was tall and the beautiful was beautiful, and the not-tall was

---

[2] It will be my view that this can be done except in cases where x and not-x (when x and not-x are incompatibles) are predicated of one and the same subject at the same time in the same sense and same respect; for only then will the incompatibility become operative, and we cannot "remain unscathed" (cp. p. 115 f. below).
[3] Accepting Cornford's (1935) reading, p. 292 n. 1.

not-tall, and the not-beautiful was not-beautiful, so not-being was and is not-being, a kind with a nature of its own. (cp. n. 5 below).

While the Stranger had previously argued from whole to part, from the being of difference to the being of not-x (258 A9, p. 81), he now argues from part to whole, from the being (*ousia*) of not-x to the *ousia* of not-being. Moreover, not-x and x are closely aligned in (1) and more particularly (3),[4] and there is thus a double suspicion. The Stranger may after all treat the not-x as "a single kind" with specific content like the x, and he even seems to suggest that not-being, a nature of its own, has specific content in being constituted by not-x's. But the nature of not-being is the different, and not the things which are different from any given x. Has Plato crossed the meta-line, perhaps never drawn with sufficient sharpness? For it looks as though he conceives here of not-being as qualitatively the same as the extensions of being, *to on kai to pan*, for he conceives of it by analogy with the beautiful – "as the beautiful is beautiful." What he should have said, and in fact will presently add (258 E1, p. 85 below), is that the extensions of not-being and being coincide;[5] for his purpose undoubtedly was to accord not-being the same fullness as being. And this is a significant addition to the position previously reached.

---

[4] Cp. Peck (1962) p. 64 on the parallel treatment of the not-beautiful and the beautiful. I do not agree with Peck's conclusion that *neither* is a form.

[5] Unless this was Plato's position, proposition (4), p. 83 would be a series of uninformative identical statements of the "late learner" sort. This is avoided if the subject-terms are understood extensionally, and the predicates in the intensional sense. I don't think Plato on this occasion is guilty of self-predication since there is no suggestion here that he thought of the subject-terms as paradigms.

§ 20. The very great Kinds – Conclusion: 258C–259D

The Stranger now takes leave of Parmenides, putting on record his disobedience to the latter's prohibition, never to trespass into the domain of not-being. Indeed he has gone further. Not only has he shown that things that are-not, are, he has brought to light the true nature of not-being: the different,

which is parcelled out over the whole field of things that are (*onta*) with reference to one another; and of every part of it that is set in contrast to that which is, we have dared to say that it is that which is-not (258 E1–3).

It is in this passage that the Stranger makes it clear that the "parts" of difference (the not-x's) have to be understood as its extensions, co-existent with the extensions of being (see p. 83 f. above).

He then proceeds to summarize the positions[1] for which he has argued (258 E6–259 B6):

(i) What is-not, understood as what is different, is not the contrary of what is. The contrary of what is, *to medamos on* (the Parmenidean not-being) is not a subject suitable for discussion, and was long ago dismissed from the enquiry (§4).

(ii) The kinds combine with one another. (That some kinds, e.g. motion and rest will not combine is here not repeated).

(iii) Being and difference pervade all kinds.

(iv) Being and difference pervade one another:

  (a) Difference by partaking of being *is* by virtue of that participation.

  (b) Difference is *not* that being (i.e. being itself) of which it partakes, but is different.[2]

  (c) Consequently and necessarily difference is a thing that is-not.

  (d) Being itself, on the other hand, partakes of difference, and by virtue of that participation is different from all the other kinds, and consequently is not any one of them nor all of them put together.

  (e) Being then is only itself (i.e. it is its single self, cp. 257 A4–6, p. 77 above).

(v) All the other kinds, whether taken severally or all together, in many respects are and in many respects are-not (cp. 256 E5 f., p. 76 above).

---

[1] These will in subsequent sections be referred to as the "ontological pattern."

[2] This once again is a case of unavoidable self-predication, more glaring on Plato's analysis:

It seems striking that in this summary only two of the five great kinds are mentioned; not only have motion and rest been quietly dropped, but sameness too is absent, except for an indirect reference in (iv e). There may be two reasons for this. Firstly, I believe that being and difference have a part to play in the account of true and false *logos* that is to follow, while the other three have not. So the present passage serves as a transition to the next section. Secondly, it seems that Plato has come to realize that being and difference, and that means being and not-being, are the most important instruments in his quintet. Since the only sameness he acknowledges is sameness in relation to self, sameness does not appear to be an independent binder of forms, but comes as a correlate of difference. Motion and rest, on the other hand, are not at the same level as the other three. They are attributes, not formal determinants, of what is, and this may explain why they have been left behind on reaching the apex of the dialogue. On my reading, the present passage bears witness to a persistent tendency in Plato towards economy in explanatory notions and concentration on as few ultimate principles as possible (cp. p. 3).

Lastly, it will have become obvious that the relations between being and difference, since they pervade one another, are symmetrical, and this by implication applies to their relations with sameness as well. Cornford, then, was right as far as these "forms of forms" were concerned (cp. p. 46 above). He was wrong, however, as we have shown, as far as the relations of motion and rest with being are concerned (p. 41 f.), for while they partake of being, being does not participate in them, so that these relations must be asymmetrical. And it seems plausible that the same holds concerning motion and rest in their relation to sameness and difference, although we have no explicit evidence in this case.

This concludes our discussion of the very great kinds.

"difference participates in difference in relation to being." Moreover the subject term has here to be taken as *auto kath hauto* – for a similar case see p. 75 above – which is inconsistent with the earlier argument that difference is always *pros allo* (cp. p. 71).

§ 21. The Problem of Falsity and the Possibility of Discourse[1]: 259D–261C

From Parmenides back to the Sophist! We must not overlook our over-all aim to define the Sophist. At one time we thought to have pinned him down as a fabricator of falsehoods, of deceptive semblances, but then we came up against the difficulty, how anything could seem to be without really being, or how one was able to say something which yet was not true (236 E, p. 13). For the Sophist had shielded behind Parmenidean not-being, and argued that to say what is false is to say what is-not.[2] But what is-not cannot be; it is unthinkable and unutterable. Therefore it is (logically) impossible for any statement to be false. All statements must be true, and consequently we cannot unmask the Sophist as a deceiver. This position is now recalled: deception depends upon the possibility of falsity (260 C6).

But meanwhile Plato has been able to show that being and not-being pervade one another, and thereby has breached the Sophist's defences; for if to say what is false, is to say what is-not, and what is-not in a way *is*, then falsehoods are thinkable and utterable, and semblances and deceit may thrive. But there still remains the question: in what sense is his account of the being of not-being applicable to discourse, and more particularly false discourse? For that account was an ontological one. It served him well in the world of forms, the world of the beautiful, the tall and the just. But *logos* has a nature of its own, distinct from the nature of everything else. It occupies a different dimension, as it were. What, then, is the link between the nature of discourse and the ontological pattern which has been established, as summarized in the preceding section? Shall we be justified in saying, for instance, that a false statement is related to a true one, as the not-x's are to the x's,

---

[1] *Logos*, which will be rendered as "discourse" or "statement" according to context.
[2] Plato accepts this definition of false statement. Cp. the Stranger's own definitions, p. 21 with note 2, above.

the not-beautiful to the beautiful? Although Plato in his *megista gene* arguments could not but express himself by means of *logoi*, the nature of *logos qua logos* was not at issue. But it is now, and Plato, while not asking questions as I have put them shows himself aware that discourse poses problems peculiar to itself.

This becomes manifest in, among other things, the choice of his key examples by reference to which true and false are to be explained: "Theaetetus sits" and "Theaetetus flies." They are of the simplest and briefest kind (262 C6), "primitive" statements, we may call them. Moreover they are statements about a particular, thus could not in any way have formed part of his meta-arguments which went before. It would have been easy enough for Plato to make up a false proposition about forms, such as might occur in the course of a division through insufficient attention to precise degrees of resemblance and dissimilarity (cp. *Phaedr.* 262A) or by mistaking one form for another (*Soph.* 253 D1 f.). Such an example would have been instructive for his students in dialectic, and fitted in well with his ever present educational concern. It looks, then, as though Plato was intent on stripping his examples to a bare minimum, as well as avoiding any suggestion of doctrinal reference, which might make it more difficult for us to discern the nature of true and false statement *qua se*.[3]

The argument begins with an obvious reference to the "late learners" who did not allow for synthetic statements (pp. 44, 47 f. above) and thus "separated everything from every other thing" (259 D9 f.). Their position is relevant to the present enquiry into the possibility of false statement, for as pointed out earlier, by only admitting tautologies these men reduced discourse to a level at which no information whatever, either true or false, could be conveyed. The Stranger next states three positions:

A. The separation of each thing from everything else is tantamount to a complete abolition of all discourse (259 E4 f.).[4]

B. For discourse has come to us through (*dia*) (owes its existence to) the weaving together (*symploke*) of the forms with one another (259 E5 f.).

C. [in slight paraphrase] It was in good time, then, that we forced those "separatists" to admit that forms mingle with one another, for we have thus secured the position that discourse is one of the kinds that are (260 A1–6).

---

[3] Other factors which may have contributed to Plato's choice of the two examples will become apparent as we go along. It should be noted that what Plato has to say about *logos* in the remaining sections of the dialogue applies equally to thinking and belief (*dianoia* and *doxa*). Thinking is a silent discourse of the soul with itself, and the beliefs entertained as the result of that discourse are unvocalized *logoi* (263 E, cp. *Theaet.* 189 E f. and p. 20 above).

[4] This is presently expanded by the remark: "to rob us of discourse is to rob us of philosophy" (260 A6 f.).

The crucial and most widely debated statement is B, which establishes the link between discourse and the "ontological pattern." As the Stranger's point of departure is the doctrine of the "late learners" that only identical, i.e. no synthetic statements, are possible, we must look at the earlier passage in which their position was refuted. For there too a connection between the combination of forms and discourse was affirmed. The conclusion was that the discourse we have (and that means our synthetic statements) is incompatible with a denial of the combination of forms so that any attempt to put that denial into words will be self-refuting: "The foe is in their own household" (252 C6 f.). The Stranger now goes beyond what he had then argued, affirming that the discourse we have depends for its very being on the interweaving of forms. This implies at least this, that if there was no plurality of intermingling forms, if the universe was Parmenidean, or a late learner's paradise (i.e. constituted by unrelated Parmenidoid characters), then there could be no discourse.[5]

But the "precise sense and precise respect" in which the interweaving of the forms with one another has to be understood in relation to discourse is difficult to make out. As far as I can see, there are three alternative ways in which B has been interpreted:

I. The Stranger may wish to affirm that because the forms combine, it is possible to combine a subject and a predicate in a statement, i.e. to make genuine predications, such as the "late learners" denied.

II. The Stranger may wish to say that all discourse exemplifies a weaving together of forms. In making a statement we combine forms, and we can only make statements because forms are capable of combining. The weaving of forms actually occurs in the statement.

III. It is possible to understand B in the light of C. Because forms combine with one another, the form "discourse" combines with the form "being," and therefore "discourse" is one of the kinds that are.

In assessing the relative merits of these three interpretations, we must, I think, bear in mind the purpose of this and the following sections, which is to establish the possibility of false statement. Therefore, when the Stranger asserts that discourse has come to us through the weaving together of the forms with one another, it seems reasonable to take

---

[5] Plato was surely right in holding that there could be no significant discourse in a world which was either completely fused or completely disjointed – though there could still be discourse in the sense of "mere names." On the other hand *we* might only admit a link between discourse and our *understanding* of reality, which would allow for alternatives. That is to say, given the discourse we have, the world might just as well be Aristotelean in character as Platonic or anything else, provided it was *at some level* constituted by a plurality of interconnected *onta*.

discourse as referring to both true and false statements. Since to affirm what is false, is to affirm what is not – and this definition will presently be repeated (260 C3 f.) – the weaving of forms would include their interweaving with not-being (difference), and therefore involve a reference to the meta-arguments about the *megista gene*. On this line of reasoning, the reference to B would include items (iii) and (iv) of the "ontological pattern."

Thus viewed, *Interpretation I*, which takes B as exclusively directed against the "late learners", seems too narrow. It is plausible enough in controverting their position which has just been restated, but does not materially go beyond arguments put forward by the Stranger when he first introduced the combination of forms; unless forms combined, all ontological statements made by ourselves and previous philosophers would be meaningless. This indeed does give us a sense in which discourse depends on the interweaving of forms. Moreover, Interpretation I would also account for the paradigm true statement "Theaetetus sits": we can make this predication, because the form man combines with "sitting" in the sense that man is the kind of creature that has the capacity to sit, and Theaetetus is a man (participates in the form man).[6] But by restricting the significance of B to item (ii) of the "ontological pattern" (p. 85) it fails to take false *logos* in its purview. It blankets the *megista gene* section, and does not throw any light on C. Therefore, although something like Interpretation I may possibly have been in Plato's mind, it cannot be all that he had in mind.

We turn to *Interpretation II* that the interweaving of forms actually takes place in each and every statement we make.[7] In naming the constituents of a statement we refer to the forms for which these constituents stand. The interweaving of forms is not a precondition of stating or believing, to state or believe *is* to interweave forms. This would not preclude that statements may ostensibly be about particulars, but any statement about particulars necessarily connects forms. Discourse, on this view, owes its being to the weaving of forms only in the sense that there can be no discourse without weaving actually

---

[6] Following Peck (1962) p. 53 we may wonder whether Plato thought at all of combinations of this type since they are *in toto* different from the sort of combinations he has been concerned with throughout the dialogue. I should not, however, call it an "anomaly" (Peck), given his down to earth example "Theaetetus sits."

[7] Interpretations of this type, though not necessarily the same as the one given here, have been put forward by Bluck (1957) and Gulley (1962). I refer to summaries and criticisms by Peck (1962) and Lorenz and Mittelstrass (1966).

taking place, not in the sense that there is an independent ontological pattern of *symploke* which is the rationale of discourse in general.

Interpretation II can be supported by the following considerations:

(i) In the next section (§ 22) the Stranger will point out that a meaningful statement is complex, interweaving (*symplekon*) noun with verb, that is, he will use the same term *symploke* of speech elements as he uses in B of forms. This term occurred only once before but was absent from the *megista gene* sections. One may be tempted to infer that in any ordinary meaningful statement the interweaving of speech elements signifies an interweaving of forms. Moreover, the Stranger is going to invoke the letter analogy for the combination of speech elements, as he invoked it earlier for the combination of forms.

(ii) After the Stranger has introduced his two examples and given his definitions of true and false statement, he will with reference to what has been asserted of Theaetetus (viz. sitting and flying respectively), make the following point:

For we said that in the case of everything there are many things that are, many that are not (263 B11 f.).

This refers back to the conclusion concerning forms at 256 E5 f. (p. 76). It is here ostensibly applied to a particular, Theaetetus, or is it? May the Stranger's remark perhaps indicate that in speaking of Theaetetus it was forms he had in mind?

Interpretation II has to contend with the following difficulties:

(a) If the interweaving of forms takes place *in* the statement, it is surely not enough that they are implicitly referred to, we have a right to expect that terms standing for forms actually occur in the statement. But there is only one such term present in each of the paradigm examples (viz. "sitting" and "flying") which has been considered as doing duty for a form since many things can share in it. But we need at least two forms in each statement for the interweaving of forms *with one another* (*allelon*) to take place. Where is the second form?

Moravcsic (1960) p. 127 pointed to the copula as signifying the second form, namely the "form of relational being," and he would wish to understand "Theaetetus sits" as "Sitting is in relation to Theaetetus." But not only have we found Moravcsic's view unacceptable on general grounds (p. 69 f.), there *is* no copula in the two statements concerned. The only other candidate for interweaving is the subject term: in interweaving the noun Theaetetus with the verb "sits", we interweave *ipso facto*, we may be told, the form man with the form sitting. On Interpretation I, too, it could be held that this was the interweaving referred to, but there was no difficulty then, because according to that interpretation, the interweaving did not take place *in* the statement. Interpretation II, however, requires that we somehow identify the particular Theaetetus with the form man. A justification for this move may be found in Hamlyn (1955) who pointed out that Plato did not recognize proper names in our sense but only names of forms.[8] It is of course true that on Plato's philosophical analysis a particular can only be understood in terms of the forms in which it participates, but there must still be a significant difference between naming as subject term a particular and naming a form in which it participates, for it participates in many forms. As argued earlier, Plato could have named a form, but did not. Interestingly enough, in the section on the weaving of speech elements already referred to (§ 22) the Stranger will choose as his example "A man understands," i.e. he names the form "man" as his subject term. I have given reasons why Plato may have preferred examples of true and false statement which ostensibly steered clear of his ontological doctrines (p. 88). After his explication of the nature of discourse (§ 22) the Stranger introduces his examples with the words: "Now let us fix our attention on ourselves" (262 E10), thus returning to the actual dramatic situation. Indeed, he adds at one point: "Theaetetus whom I am talking to at this moment" (263 A8), and Theaetetus again will say: "The statement belongs to *me* and is about *me*." Interpretation II misjudges, I believe, the element of common-sense realism which is involved in the choice of the Stranger's examples – whatever his analysis of what we designate as "proper names". It also shows itself unaware of the liberalisation which has taken place in the *Sophist* where Plato accepts particulars as *onta qua* particulars.[9]

[8] "... words like 'Socrates,' 'man,' or 'good,' as used in sentences, are all alike to be interpreted as referring to forms ... 'Socrates' is, to use the more modern idiom of Russell, a disguised description, in that it unpacks into a list of all the forms in which Socrates partakes" (p. 294 f.).

[9] Prauss (1966) pp. 188 ff., favouring Interpretation II, would agree that Plato in the *Sophist* no longer considers particulars as bundles of *dynameis* (which are knowable in terms of forms), but posits individual things as "the same" (*tauton touto*, 251 A6) and as "one," of which we speak by many names (251 B2 f.). In so far as we make specific determinations of Theaetetus, i.e. speak of him by many names (e.g. "sits"), we posit him as "one" and as "the same," and hence it is the *noëma* (thought) of the form sameness which is combined in our *logoi* with other *noëmata*, namely with our thoughts of the specific determinations that are in question. According to this variant of Interpretation II the *symploke* which is supposed to take place in a *logos* is not, as affirmed in B, of forms, but of thoughts of forms. Although "the same" does not occur *in* the statement, in ascribing specific determinations to Theaetetus we cannot but think him "as the same." Prauss supports his Copernican revolution by

(b) A second objection is this: if forms are interwoven *in* statements and beliefs, then their mutual participation, prior to statements being uttered or beliefs being entertained, exists only as a possibility. Interpretation II comes dangerously close to reversing the connection affirmed in B: it is not discourse that owes its existence to the interweaving of forms with one another, rather it is the latter that comes into being in discourse. But that ontology is prior to statement is not only indicated in B but has been consistently maintained throughout the dialogue.[10] Upholders of Interpretation II might retort that the underlying ontological relations are compatibilities (in the present case between man and sitting) from which we choose in producing actual weavings in our statements. But the properties of kinds, e.g. man's capacity to sit are anchored in, and part of, their natures. In stating them we do not *make* them actual but affirm what *is* actual. While the weaving of speech elements is, the weaving of forms is not, in our power. "The *symploke* of *eide*," Peck (1962) pointed out, "is beyond our control; some blend, some do not; we merely recognize it when it is there" (p. 59 n. 1).

(c) Interpretation II ignores Plato's concern in the present sections to show that false statements are possible, i.e. that they say something (*legein ti*), are not meaningless. Hence he cannot merely mean by B that a form signified by the subject term is interwoven with the form signified by the verb. For in the Stranger's example of a false statement – Theaetetus flies – it clearly is not. But the Stranger will not say that the false statement is false because we have interwoven incorrectly: for forms interwoven "incorrectly" are not interwoven at all, and that

two subsidiary arguments: (i) Since thought consists of silent *logoi* (see p. 88 n. 3) *logos* is formulated thought. In speaking we don't only talk but also think. Hence *logoi* do not merely combine words but also thoughts (*noëmata*). The *symploke* of speech elements becomes thus a symbolic expression of a *symploke* of *noëmata*. (ii) The Stranger in announcing his examples says that he is going to "put together a thing (*pragma*) with an action (*praxis*) by means of an *onoma* and a *rema*" (262 E 12 f.). In a number of places Plato uses the term *pragma* to distinguish a form from its *onoma*. Hence *pragma* stands for the thought of a form as distinct from naming it, and in the present case that form is sameness as distinct from the name – Theaetetus (!).

Prauss' attempt to account for B, involves a two-fold reduction. It reduces the *symploke* of forms to a *symploke* of thoughts, and the thought of Theaetetus to the thought of the transcendental condition of thinking Theaetetus. It is at variance with the fundamental approach of the present study, and objection (b) which follows applies to its treatment as well. On forms as *noëmata* see § 1, p. 2.

Concerning (i): Plato's view of thinking as unvocalised discourse does not allow us to draw any conclusions regarding the thinking that may, or may not, accompany vocalised discourse. Concerning (ii), the term *pragma* is topic neutral, corresponding roughly to the Latin *res*. It may, but need not, refer to forms.

[10] See e.g. pp. 48, 49, 53, 59, 66 f. above.

again, on the strength of B, would mean that no statement has been produced. We have said nothing (*ouden legein*), and the possibility of false statement has not been established.

As pointed out (p. 89 f.) the significance of B must be sought just in this, that it gives us the condition of true as well as false discourse. And it can only account for the latter by bringing the form of difference (not-being) into the *symploke*. And this in fact will be the Stranger's procedure. But that form does not occur *in* the statement, it is not signified by any of its constituent elements. And this, I think is fatal to Interpretation II.

Interpretation III was suggested by Peck. It removes – perhaps too radically – "man," "sitting" and "flying" from the purview of B and brings the *megista gene* arguments back into the picture. Because forms combine, the form "discourse" can combine with being, and therefore "discourse" is one of the kinds that are (C).[11] According to this interpretation, then, we are concerned with the formal determination of discourse, not of its possible contents. But to say of anything that it participates in (combines with) being is not to determine it completely. Interpretation III, though on the right track, has stopped too soon. In order to appraise B and C fully, we have to draw on the conclusions at which we arrived as a result of the *megista gene* arguments, and note that two further determinations are necessarily involved:

(a) Whatever participates in being must have a nature of its own (cp. p. 69 on "being as").

(b) Whatever participates in being must also participate in difference, i.e. not-being (p. 76 f., cp. 258 E1–3, p. 85).

Accordingly it is the *symploke* of being with not-being, and therefore of discourse with both, i.e. items (iii) and (iv) of the ontological pattern, which is referred to in B.[12] Interestingly enough, in the only other passage where we met with the term *symploke*, it was also used of being and not-being (240 C1, p. 18 f.). That being and not-being pervade one another would thus appear to be the ultimate rationale of reality as well as discourse.

Plato shows himself aware of both conditions (a) and (b), and this

---

[11] Discourse is spoken of as both a form and a kind (260 A5, 260 D5 ff.).

[12] I feel confident that this is what was foremost in Plato's mind, but would not deny that he may *also* have thought of the combination of forms at large, i.e. of item (ii) for this much is suggested by the immediately preceding reference to the "separatists." In any case, there is not in his thinking as tidy a divide as we may wish for, between forms and meta-forms (cp. p. 56), although we have seen that his arguments pivot on this distinction.

provides strong support for Interpretation III. As soon as the Stranger has affirmed that discourse is one of the kinds that are, he says:

Moreover we need at the present moment come to an agreement about the nature of discourse (*ti pot' estin*) (260 A7 f.).

This, as already indicated, will be discussed in the next section (§ 22). Questioned by Theaetetus, why we must proceed in this way, the Stranger reintroduces the subject of not-being, recalling that it is a single kind among the others, dispersed over the whole field of *onta* (260 B7–8). He then points out that we have to consider whether "it blends with discourse and thinking" (B10–11) for "if it does not blend, everything must be true" (C1–2). The definition that to think or say what is-not amounts to falsity in thought and speech, is then repeated (C3–4). The gist of the argument is that the possibility of false statements depends on the mingling of discourse with not-being.

Now since discourse is considered a form or kind, and all kinds blend with not-being – for "not-being was found to have its share in being" (260 D5) – we may wonder why the blending of discourse with not-being should still be open to question. We need to remember here the basic position that some forms blend, while some do not, i.e. are incompatible, where incompatibility is due to the nature of the forms concerned; e.g. it is in virtue of their own natures that motion and rest cannot blend with one another. As mentioned earlier, Plato is aware that discourse, though one of the kinds that are, holds a special place among them. Its nature may be such as to make it impossible for it to blend with not-being. And if this were so, then it would indeed be impossible to say what is false. The Sophist will be quick to espy this escape route; almost aping the conclusion reached at 252 E1–2 (p. 51), he may contend that

somef orms partake of not-being, some do not, and discourse and thinking are among those that do not (260 D6–8).

If he were to make good this claim, he could start all over again, and deny that there can be such things as images and semblances, and hence we should not have caught him after all. His denial that the form discourse can combine with not-being is his last line of defence.

Issue (a) and (b) thus hang together. The investigation of the nature of discourse is required in order to establish that it is not such as to preclude its combination with not-being (cp. 261 C6–9).

As an afterthought we may wonder why Plato did not attempt to treat falsity as a purely semantic problem. Why invoke ontology? There seem to be a number of reasons.

(1) The denial of the possibility of false *logos* arose from an ontological root, i.e. from Parmenides' philosophy of being. It therefore would seem reasonable, if not necessary, to effect a cure of the disease at its root level.

(2) For Plato meaning does not only depend on the nature of discourse, i.e. on the structure of speech elements in a statement (to be set out presently), though this is certainly a necessary condition. It also depends on the order of reality which discourse reflects, and to which it refers. The aspect of that order which was of interest to Plato in his earlier work was participation in substantive forms. In the *Sophist* it has shifted to meta-formal conditions, i.e. to the ontological pattern that has been mapped out by the interrelations of the very great kinds. What interests him now is not so much the old question: Is "Theaetetus sits" true, and therefore meaningful because Theaetetus participates in the form man, and the form man in sitting? Rather it is the question: Is "Theaetetus flies," meaningful though false, because the form discourse combines with not-being?

(3) Since for Plato the problem of falsity or saying what is-not, is basically the problem of the being of not-being, he will naturally feel inclined to apply to it the kind of solution which he used with regard to "words pronounced after the prefix not" (257 B10 ff., p. 81), that is to say, he will want to treat what is false on the lines of the "not-beautiful". On the other hand, it is not my view that Plato included discourse among the kinds that are, i.e. made it part of the ontological pattern, merely in order to apply that sort of treatment. But while he approached the problem of false statements at the ontological level, his choice of examples – whatever else may have prompted it – testifies to his conviction that his solution is applicable to discourse in general.

Lastly we need to guard against a possible misconception. Since the participation of discourse in not-being is required to account for falsity, we may be tempted to conclude that its participation in being might account for truth. There is in Greek thinking a natural affinity between being and truth, but this is breaking up in the *Sophist* (cp. pp. 13, 18 above). Just as what is-not has a share in being, so what-is has a share in not-being. Thus a false statement participates both in not-being and in being: it is really and truly (*ontos kai alethos*) a false statement (263 D4). And there will also emerge an important sense, in which a true statement participates in not-being (difference) as well as in being. At the moment it may suffice to point out that Plato seemed to consider it as of the utmost calamity if every statement was true, realizing perhaps that if all statements are true none can be true.

§ 22. The Nature of Logos: 261C–262E

In explaining the nature of *logos*, the Stranger must convince the Sophist that it is possible for a statement to blend with not-being, which means that it is possible to say what is-not (*legein ta me onta*). Under which condition would that not be possible?

We need to remember the arguments about motion and rest. If motion were to blend with rest, it would become *stasimos* (stationary), i.e. be forced to change its nature into that of its opposite and thereby become its opposite (255 AII ff., p. 59). Its very nature would have been corrupted, and we may therefore raise the question whether the nature of discourse might be similarly corrupted by blending with not-being. Now, given the "ontological pattern," without which there would be no discourse at all, the specific nature of the kind *logos* is such as to enable us to say something (*legein ti*). This, as was pointed out earlier, is equivalent to saying something meaningful, speaking sense, while its opposite *legein meden*, to say nothing, is equivalent to saying something meaningless, speaking non-sense. The problem then is, can *logos* combine with not-being, i.e. say *ta me onta*, without thereby becoming its opposite, in the sense that its nature would be corrupted from *legein ti* to *legein meden*? Does *logos* when false cease to be *logos*?

In enquiring into the nature of discourse the Stranger will lay bare the conditions of *legein ti*,[1] but he does so with the explicit purpose of showing that *logos qua logos* remains unaffected by *legein la me onta*; i.e. by saying what is false. It would therefore appear that, as against the Sophist, the Stranger is under obligation to establish the following points:

---

[1] The conditions of *legein ti* with which we shall be concerned are necessary, not sufficient conditions of meaning. Discourse is ultimately dependent on the "ontological pattern," but this can now remain outside our consideration.

(1) That a false *logos* does not entail that the referents of its constituent elements do not possess being; e.g. that the statement "Theaetetus flies," which is false, does not entail "Theaetetus does not exist," which would make the statement self-contradictory and therefore meaningless.

(2) That there is a legitimate distinction between a false *logos* and a meaningless string of words, where each word has reference in its own right.

(3) That the falsity of a *logos* does not entail that what it asserts is in no way whatsoever, i.e. is *medamos on* which, the Stranger would have to agree, can neither be thought nor be uttered (cp § 4).

Plato regards meaningful statement as a complex unit, a "whole of parts." In order to elucidate its structure, the Stranger recalls what had been ascertained concerning letters and forms: some fit, some do not. The combination of words (signs of speech) in a statement is analogous to the combination of vowels and consonants in words. A meaningful statement is *dependent* on their fitness to combine (262 D9 f.).[2] As already mentioned, two types of constituent element are distinguished, *onoma* and *rema*, which are fit to combine and make a statement. *Onoma* means "name," "word" or "noun," *rema* may be rendered as "what is said." These terms do not, however, correspond to our "subject" and "predicate", since usages of both for either occur. Although the distinction is a logical rather than a grammatical one,[3] the customary translations "noun" and "verb" should be accepted on the strength of the Stranger's explicit definitions: *rema* is a sign applied to actions, *onoma* to what performs those actions (262 A3–7). Both are introduced as "signs used in speech to signify being (*ousia*)" (261 E5 f.), which we may interpret as: both *onoma* and *rema*, *qua* constituent elements of a statement refer to something that is, a position which the Sophist would surely accept, at least as long as we do not claim that a statement might be false. This leads to the first point which the Stranger has to establish, namely

(1) that the being of that, to which the elements of a statement refer, is unaffected by its falsity. Common terms would cause him no trouble, since these refer to forms, and forms possess being, no matter whether or not anything participates in them at any given time. Words referring to particulars – such as Theaetetus in the subsequent examples – are more problematic, and here the Stranger seems to have three lines of defence. (i) In uttering the false statement "Theaetetus flies", he will add, as already mentioned, "Theaetetus whom I am talking to

---

[2] At 261 D8 ff., the Stranger suggests that meaning *indicates* that fitness, but he takes this to be Theaetetus' thinking in the matter.

[3] See Crombie (1963) p. 494 f., cp. Guthrie (1969) 220 f. Moravcsic's suggestion (1962, p. 63) that *rema* must here be understood as "description" is not supported by Plato's definitions or by examples.

now," thereby affirming that Theaetetus exists. But the Sophist would be undeterred and reply that the Stranger was contradicting himself in affirming and denying the existence of Theaetetus in one breath. (ii) The Stranger might argue *ad hominem* that the Sophist could not distinguish between a true and a meaningless statement about a deceased person who did not exist anyhow, or alternatively that all statements about deceased persons must be meaningless. That this was felt to be a problem is suggested by the Stranger's explicit assertion that a (meaningful) statement gives information about things past, present or future (262 D2 f.). (iii) Finally the Stranger points out that "a statement, if it is to be a statement, must be about something (*peri tinos*); it cannot be about nothing" (262 E5 f.), which I take to mean that the statement must refer to something that is, which would include whatever (or whoever) is denoted by the *onoma* term. The Sophist might concur and draw the conclusion that a false statement, being about nothing, is not a statement.

(2) In order to distinguish a false statement from a meaningless concatenation of words, the Stranger points out that to state is to interweave verbs with nouns. A string of verbs, e.g. "walks runs sleeps", does not signify any action performed or not performed, and similarly any string of nouns, e.g. "lion stag horse", does not signify the being of anything that is or is not (262 C).[4] I take this to mean that neither of the two types of constituent can function meaningfully in isolation from the other. The Stranger does not deny that the words, which make up these concatenations, have meaning each in itself, though he seems to suggest that this is so because they are capable of being combined with words of the other type and thus make statements. For he says that the interweaving of noun with verb as, e.g., in "a man understands" accomplishes something (*perainei ti*), we get a statement that is informative.[5] This criterion is acceptable as a necessary condition of meaning, but falls short in so far as it does not enable us to distinguish between false statements and correctly structured nonsense, and therefore would be grist for the Sophist's mill. The Stranger

[4] See Cornford (1935) p. 305 n. 1.

[5] This implies that the speech elements by themselves do not accomplish anything, that they are incomplete. We may therefore question whether Plato at the time of writing the *Sophist* still subscribed to the view expressed in the *Cratylus* (388 B f.) that names are informative as instruments for distinguishing things according to their natures. Perhaps so, as far as the names of forms are concerned, for these name natures. But even concerning forms Plato would now hold that we only obtain information (i.e. accomplish something) by stating their relations with other forms. With the shedding of the Parmenidoid form conception and the new doctrine of the communion of forms, the emphasis in language has shifted from naming to stating.

adds however that any statement must have a certain character (262 E8), meaning that it must be either true or false. This enlightened move would indeed make it possible to validly distinguish between false statements, and correctly structured non-sense which has neither character, but unfortunately, as against the Sophist, begs the question at issue.

(3) The Stranger is more successful regarding the third position. To state is not merely to give names (262 D3); that is to say, the utterance of a statement is not reducible to the utterance of its constituents (*onoma* and *rema*) each of which, taken singly, has a naming function. A statement, being a complex whole (*plegma*), does not name anything, from which it follows that a false statement does not name a non-entity (something that is in no way whatsoever), or in earlier parlance, that it is but the name of a name. The reference of a statement is not analogous to the nominee of a name. It is indirect. A statement says something *about* what is, or is becoming or has become or is to be, i.e. it makes something known, gives information (262 D2–6).[6] "About" (*peri*) is the decisive word here. The information may be false, but this leaves untouched what is or becomes or will become. Contra Parmenides and his Sophistic stepchildren, to think and to speak (and that is to state) is not to think or to speak being, it is to think and speak *about* what is (with what becomes or has not yet become thrown into the bargain). The object of thought and speech, and therefore of *logos*, is not its direct object but extrinsic to it (cp. p. 6 n. 2). The Parmenidean cramp has been loosened. Stating and its object have been differentiated from one another, and the symbiosis of being and true, and of not-being and false seems finally to dissolve. True and false are no longer viewed as a property of reality (or un-reality) but reside in statements. *Soph.* 262D anticipates Aristotle in *Metaphys.* E, IV.

Unfortunately Plato did not reap the benefit from this brilliant line of thought. If he had, he might have revised the definition, that to say what is false is *legein ta me onta*, and given up the search for an ontological justification of false *logos*. Why did he fail to do it? – Probably because he felt assured that he had already taken the lethal sting out of not-being, and thought he had to (or maybe even wished to) win final victory in the Sophist's own domain.

---

[6] Frede (1967) p. 62 f. takes this passage to refer to "expressions," to the "y" in "x is y," i.e. to predicates. But predicates (*rema* terms) signify or indicate, only the complete statement "x is y" gives information; *deloi* (262 D2) requires *logos* (C9) as its subject. Plato unfortunately will eventually sacrifice the unity of *logoi* which he here establishes, but his later move should not be read back into the present passage.

§ 23. True and False: 262E–263D

"Theaetetus sits"	*"Theaetetus flies"*
(a) The true statement says things that are (*legei ta onta*), as they are about you (*hos estin peri sou*) [i.e. about Theaetetus] (263 B4 f.).	(b) The false statement says things different from the things that are (*hetera ton onton*) (263 B7).
	(c) Accordingly it says things that are not (*legei ta me onta*) as things that are (*hos onta*) (263 B9).
	(d) But things that are (*onta*) different from things that are about you (*hetera onton peri sou*) (263 B11).
	(e) For we said that about everything (*peri hekaston*) there are many things that are (*onta*) and also many that are-not (*ouk onta*) (263 B11 f.).

In the present section I shall deal with two topics: assertion and fact, and grounds and criteria of true and false, reserving for § 24 the crucial question of the being of false *logos*.

I. ASSERTION AND FACT

Propositions (a)–(d) relate the assertions made in the two statements to the fact in virtue of which they are true and false respectively. Thus *ta onta* in (a), and *ta me onta* in (c) refer to the assertions, while *hos estin peri sou* in (a), and *hetera onton peri sou* in (d) relate what is asserted to what is the case.[1]

My next point is that the *onta* and *me onta*, which the two *logoi* say, are not merely "sitting" and "flying," not what is referred to by the two *rema* terms, but what is asserted by each *logos* as a whole, viz.

---

[1] Reading *peri sou* with *hos estin* and *hetera onton* respectively, not (contra Owen (1970) p. 264 n. 76) with *legei*. Accordingly *hos* is rendered as "as", not "that". There will be further discussion of propositions (b) and (c) in § 24. On *hos* = "as" in Plato cp. Kahn (1966) p. 253 n. 5.

"Theaetetus sits" and "Theaetetus flies."[2] Plato takes *logos* as a unity, and therefore can treat it as a kind or form. While it is a complex unity, a whole of parts (as all forms are), it only says something (*legein ti*) as a *symploke* of *onoma* and *rema*. Its function, as has been made clear in the preceding section, is distinct from that of its constituent elements. It says; they name, indicate, signify.

Consequently, when the Stranger calls the *onta*, affirmed by the two *logoi*, "as they are about you" in (a), and "different from things that are about you" in (d), the expression "about you" (*peri sou*) must be taken to refer to the actually present Theaetetus, as an aspect of the facts, while the two phrases in which the *peri sou* occurs relate what has been asserted to the verifying/falsifying fact of which the actually present Theaetetus is one aspect.[3]

The ground for the distinction, and therefore the relation between what is the case and what is asserted has been prepared by the important passage 262 D2–6 (see p. 101 and n. 3 below), as well as by the conversation that follows it. The Stranger, as already mentioned (p. 92) returns to the actual dramatic situation, and says these things to Theaetetus:

> Now let us fix our attention on ourselves . . .
> I will make a statement to you . . .
> You are to tell me what the statement is about . . .
> It is for you to say what it is about – to
> whom it belongs.

Theaetetus replies with reference to the true statement:

> Clearly about me: it belongs to me,

and with reference to the false one:

> That too can only be described as belonging
> to me and about me. (262 E–263 A)

---

[2] Contra Hackforth (1945) p. 58, it is not the *rema* which is true or false but the statement (cp. 262 E5–8, 263 A11 ff.). We may remember the question, "Can *logos* blend with not-being, can it say what is false?" So obviously, it is not "flying" that must blend with not-being, that can say what is false. It is "Theaetetus flies." Cp. Gilbert Ryle (1966) p. 282 f.

[3] "Things that are about you" in [(a), (d)] links up with *peri tinos* (262 E5, p. 100) and parallels 262 D2 f. (p. 101) where the Stranger points out that a statement gives information *about* (*peri*) what is or is becoming etc. What *is* or is different about the actually present Theaetetus is the fact about which the two statements purport to give information, and in virtue of which they are true and false respectively.

Why that persistent effort to bring home to us that the two statements are about Theaetetus when he has ostensibly been named as their subject term? In my view it is the Stranger's wish to differentiate between assertion and fact, between the contents of the two *logoi* and the live actuality of his respondent, Theaetetus.[4] There seem to be three reasons for this: (i) He points to the actual Theaetetus in order to underscore that the false statement he has made about him does not entail an affirmation of his non-existence (p. 99 f. above). (ii) He makes sure that both statements are about the same person, forestalling a move by the Sophist to accept "Theaetetus flies" as a true statement about another Theaetetus. (iii) He relates the statements to what is the case, as the source of their respective truth and falsity, and without differentiation there could be no relation. While in one sense a statement is "about" its subject, in the sense that matters here it is "about" the complex fact into which the subject enters as one of its elements.

II. GROUNDS AND CRITERIA OF TRUE AND FALSE

Perhaps we can now fully appreciate the common-sense realism involved in Plato's choice of examples. He wanted to demonstrate *ad oculos* the fact *about* which he was going to make his statements. And he wanted the true statement to be obviously true, and the false one to be palpably false. Since the two statements were chosen about one and the same state of affairs – Theaetetus "acting" here now – it is not surprising that they make contrary assertions. They are *pantapasi* (altogether) different. Sitting and flying are incompatible when affirmed of the same person in the same respect and at the same time,[5] in fact as incompatible as rest and motion, of which they are subspecies. This incompatibility, which has been built into the two examples, cannot in my view be dismissed as accidental. The two examples do not merely illustrate an already complete theory, but are a necessary part of it, and this is quite unique in the Platonic *corpus*.

We shall come back to the role of incompatibility but first will consider the question, what it is that makes the true statement true and the false one false. This involves the question of criteria, which is not, as such, raised in the dialogue, i.e. the question as to how we know

---

[4] "Theaetetus, whom I am talking to at this moment, flies," at first sight may appear to blur this differentiation. Not, however, when it is realized that the parenthetical "whom I am talking to . . ." is not part of the assertion but refers to the dramatic situation.

[5] I hope I shall be forgiven for leaving twentieth century airplane passengers out of consideration.

that the true statement is true and the false statement false.[6] Our discussion on this issue is not helped by the fact that in the present case the true statement is obviously true, and the false one palpably false, for Plato's solution had to be generally applicable in order to silence the Sophist.

There are three views to consider: (1) the view of correct and incorrect combination, (2) the correspondence/non-correspondence view, and (3) the likeness/semblance view. There are pros and cons in respect of each of these views, and it is not easy to come to a decision.

(1) This is the most advanced view, which can be found in Aristotle, and may appropriately be put in more modern terms: the true statement is true because it attaches a predicate to a subject which belongs to that subject, and the other is false because it attaches a predicate to a subject, which does not belong to it. This view has been championed, among others, by Lorenz and Mittelstrass (1966) who couch it in the terminology of *zukommen* and *zusprechen*.[7] It at once brings back position B (§ 21) and the relation between the *symploke* of forms and the *symploke* of speech elements. Both the true and the false statement obey the rules of the latter, and therefore have meaning. One of them is true because the forms associated with its speech elements combine with one another, while the other is false, because there is no combination of forms corresponding to that of its speech elements. Theaetetus, a man, does not participate in flying. Hence the ascription of flying to Theaetetus is false. The combination of subject and predicate is incorrect.

In discussing B, I gave reasons for holding that what Plato had primarily in mind was what I called the "ontological pattern," the *symploke* of being and not-being, and of discourse with both, i.e. the meta-formal conditions of discourse in general, not the specific conditions of any given statement. But the possibility that the combination of specific forms was also referred to, could not be ruled out (see p. 94 n. 12). Moreover the present view is not committed to Interpretation II of position B which we found wanting. It is committed, however, to include at least one metaform, namely difference or not-being among the *eide* whose *symploke* is to account for truth and falsity. For the incorrect combination of subject and predicate, on Plato's

---

[6] It seems that if our two questions were put to Plato, his answers would coalesce in so far as the reason why a statement is true or false would for him also be the reason why it can be known to be true or false.

[7] In the discussion that follows I am not, however, reproducing their views.

account, must be expressed in terms of the subject's participation in difference towards the predicate. It is of course the *logos* as a whole that is true or false, and which when false mingles with not-being, i.e. according to proposition (b) and (d), participates in difference in relation to what actually is the case. What the view under consideration comes to, is that the relation of difference between statement and fact is due to a relation of difference between subject and predicate. "Theaetetus flies" is false because the nominee of the *onoma* term, Theaetetus participates in difference towards flying.

The strongest support for the combination/non-combination view comes from proposition (e), for here we cannot take *onta* and *ouk onta* as referring to the complex fact. The reason is that (e) is a generalization from an earlier statement at 256E:

So in the case of every one of the forms, being is many, and not-being is infinite in number,

where "being" and "not-being" must be understood in the extensional sense (p. 76 above). The many things that are, and the infinite number of things that are-not, in the case of forms are other forms in which they participate, and in relation to which they participate in difference, and which therefore can be predicated of them, either affirmatively or negatively. Accordingly, the *onta* and *ouk onta* in (e) must also be forms in which the thing, named by the *onoma* term of a statement, participates, or in relation to which it participates in difference. The false statement, then, affirms that a thing participates in a form, while in actual fact it participates in difference in relation to it. Subject and predicate have been incorrectly combined.[8]

Although it is possible that this is what Plato had in mind, it cannot be all that he had in mind, for we still have to take into account the incompatibility which he built into his examples. Nor does (e) help us to ascertain why any given statement is false. Participation in difference has been taken *into* the statement. But a criterion for difference is still required.

---

[8] While it is obvious that *onta* in (e) refers to forms and therefore to predicates, I don't think that Lorenz and Mittelstrass (1966) are justified in making the same point concerning *onta* in proposition (a) etc. They cite as evidence passages in the *megista gene* sections where the term is used to refer to forms. But others can be found where there is no suggestion that forms are meant (e.g. 240 D–E). They qualify their view somewhat by remarking that the term is ambiguous, in so far as it may refer to particulars which exemplify forms, or to forms *qua* exemplified by particulars (excluding what they call "empty forms"). But *onta* is referentially neutral rather than ambiguous. If *onta* in *legei ta onta* in (a), referred to the predicate alone, the *logos* would not say something but merely name, and the same applies *mutatis mutandis* to (b) and (c). This surely is incompatible with 262 D2–6 (p. 101, cp. 102 f.).

The combination view can meet this requirement in the case of the example of a false statement given in our text, for the reason that "Theaetetus flies" is necessarily false. "Flying," as Stenzel (1961) pointed out, is taken from the wrong side of a division, winged animals (p. 89, Engl. ed. p. 127 f.). But Plato, to my mind, has chosen "Theaetetus flies" not because it is necessarily false, but because it is palpably false. Moreover, we are on sure ground if we take him to hold that his doctrine applies to all false statements, including those which are contingently false. For his example of a true statement, though obviously true, is contingently, not necessarily, true.

Let us now take the example of a contingently false statement, such as "Theaetetus is a shoemaker," suggested by Runciman. Everybody would agree that this is false; hence, according to Plato, it asserts things different from the things that are about Theaetetus. But what are the facts from which the assertion differs? Theaetetus is a philosopher and mathematician, we have no evidence that he has ever learned a trade, he has been seen to buy his shoes etc., etc. Yet for all we know of him, he may still secretly be making shoes. So we are really not entitled to say that the statement is false. But are we any more entitled to say that Theaetetus participates in difference with reference to shoemaking? Obviously not, since our evidence for that would have to be precisely the same. Consequently, in the case of a contingently false statement the view that falsity is due to the incorrect combination of subject and predicate, adds nothing by way of criteria to the Stranger's proposition that a false statement asserts things different from what is the case. Indeed, when the assertion is different from fact, then the combination will be incorrect, and *vice versa*. But view (1) supplies us with no criterion for either difference or incorrect combination. Nor can view (1) provide a satisfactory criterion for the true statement. It is granted that unless Theaetetus, a man, could participate in sitting, "Theaetetus sits" could not be true, so that to know which forms combine with one another, and which do not, would provide an overriding criterion of truth. But although the combination of forms is a necessary, it is not a sufficient condition. A further criterion is required, for Theaetetus may be standing (if not flying) at the time the statement is made.

(2) Cornford (1935) p. 310 f., on the strength of proposition (a), "... things that are, as they are about you," held that the truth of a statement consisted of its correspondence with the fact about Theaetetus. He took this to be the generally accepted, popular view, but

added that "*how* they correspond is not explained." However, Cornford tried to shed some light on "correspondence" by pointing out that each of the two words "Theaetetus" and "sits" "stands for one element in the complex fact. The statement as a whole is complex and its structure corresponds to the structure of the fact. Truth means this correspondence."

It is a merit of Cornford's "structural correspondence" view that it attaches to the statement as a whole, and not to the *rema* term in isolation from the subject. In this connection we may note Marten's view (1965), who does not invoke correspondence but identity; identity, however, according to him is affirmed, not between the (complex) statement and the fact, but between the predicate and the actual determination of the subject.[9] From reasons I have given (p. 102 f.), it would follow contra Marten, that however we construe the relation between assertion and fact, it is not merely the predicate that is involved. There is no *Sachverhalt* without *Sache*, no action without agent. What is made known is the fact of which both agent and action are aspects; concerning "identity" see p. 116 n. 4 below.

I would agree with Cornford that correspondence is implied in proposition (a) and accounts for the obvious truth of the primitive example in the text. But there may be difficulties in cases where the elements of the fact concerned are themselves complex, where the relation between elements of statement and elements of fact is not a one/one but a one/many relation. Plato, though, could deal with such cases by treating the *logos* concerned as a hypothesis from which he could deduce consequences until he arrived at primitive *logoi* corresponding to simple facts. How does correspondence fare in the case of the false statement? There are two possibilities. We can say that there is no fact for the statement to correspond with, but this would not help, for the Sophist would quickly retort that we have affirmed a non-existent fact, and therefore have said nothing, i.e. our allegedly false statement is meaningless: it is not a statement at all. Alternatively we may say that there is non-correspondence between the false statement and what is actually the case, and non-correspondence is obviously implied in *hetera ton onton* in propositions (b) and (d). It would not, however, work as a criterion in the case of a contingently false state-

---

[9] Marten writes: "In the true judgment the relation of subject (*onoma*) and predicate (*rema*) is simply that of *Sache* (*pragma*) and *Sachverhalt* (*praxis*) [rendered by us as "thing" and "action," p. 92f. n. 9] What is said does not "correspond" with the *Sachverhalt* i.e. the action, but declares it by comprehending predicate and actual conduct as identical; it asserts the same as the same: sitting *is* (i.e. identical with) an actual determination" (p. 171).

ment (such as "Theaetetus is a shoemaker") where we have not sufficient evidence for diagnosing non-correspondence.

(3) Although a correspondence/non-correspondence view can easily
be read off propositions (a), (b) and (d), there is evidence in the text
for yet a different view, based on the verbal image theory of language.
This was put forward in the *Cratylus* to account for the correctness of
names. Socrates compared names with pictures: they may be like or
unlike their originals (i.e. the things referred to), and therefore right or
wrong, which he assimilated to true or false (430 A ff.). The theory was
then extended to verbs, and to statements as compounds of names and
verbs (431 B f.). In our dialogue a parallel with this earlier view is
suggested by the distinction between likenesses (*eikones*) and semblances (*phantasmata*), introduced in the course of the seventh division
(§ 3). The former are exact copies of their originals,[10] the latter are
compared to the works of artists with their distortions that are to make
them seem beautiful. The Sophist is said to create semblances in
discourse, spoken images that seem to be true, and in the crucial
passage (236 E, p. 13) the Sophist's semblances are associated with
falsehoods. It is therefore reasonable to associate likeness with truth.[11]
On this view, in stating and judging we produce either likenesses or
semblances. Although the distinction between likenesses and semblances was subsequently blurred in the dialogue (p. 12), it will be
brought back shortly after the present passage, when the interrupted
seventh division is resumed (264 C f.).

What does the likeness/semblance view contribute by way of criteria
over and above the correspondence/non-correspondence view? Very
little, as far as true statements are concerned. And when the facts are
complex, it becomes even more difficult to maintain that our assertions
are "exact copies," for on this interpretation it would hardly be plausible to fall back on hypothesis and deduction. Regarding false statements, semblance is in an altogether different category from non-
correspondence. A semblance deceives and therefore in some sense or
some respect must still correspond with the facts. Semblance is not, in
an unqualified sense, other than the facts. It is certainly not an exact

---

[10] Compare the Stranger's "foremost example" of likeness-making: "creating a copy that
conforms to the proportions of the original in all three dimensions, and giving moreover the
proper colour to every part" (235 D7 ff.).

[11] This receives support from *Phil.* 38 E ff. and the simile of the internal scribe who writes
words in our soul which is compared to a book. What he writes may be either true or false
and gives rise to corresponding assertions. He is followed by a painter who creates images in
the soul of these true and false assertions.

copy but, though a distorted version, is still a version of the facts. On the strength of the analogy by which likeness and semblance-making were introduced, "Theaetetus flies" would be like an artist's rendering of the sitting Theaetetus, which is hardly credible. Perhaps Plato had at the back of his mind that "Theaetetus flying" is like a dream which Theaetetus might have of himself, "for dreamers in their sleep fancy that they have wings and are flying" (*Theaet.* 158 B3 f.). As such it might, like the Sophist's verbal images, be contrasted with the realities encountered in the actual conduct of life (234 E2). But a dream image is not a statement, although it may give rise to one.

There are two consequences which follow from the likeness/semblance view, and both militate against it:

(i) It makes truth and falsity matters of degree; for which copy is ever exact, and where does distortion begin, where does it end? "Theaetetus is lying in his grave" may be a worse distortion of the actually sitting Theaetetus than "Theaetetus flies." It is in fact a double distortion; is it twice as false?

(ii) It makes the Sophist's statements the paradigm of false statements. One may wonder what a genuine misapprehension of facts can have in common with the "insincere kind of conceited mimicry" (268 C9), practised by the Sophist. And the same question may be asked concerning the palpably false example in our text which deceives no-one. And while a contingently false statement, such as "Theaetetus is a shoemaker" may be called a semblance, if (as we might put it) it has a semblance of truth, by what token are we entitled to say that it is false?

Let us make a fresh start! It is obvious that on any view, in order to affirm truly that "Theaetetus sits," either as a spoken or an unspoken *logos*, we need to know the fact that Theaetetus is sitting. This knowledge cannot itself be propositional, cannot be of the form "Theaetetus sits," because it is the truth of "Theaetetus sits" that is at issue. It must be independent of it, and we may therefore be inclined to say, that we must perceive Theaetetus sitting in order to know that he sits. There is some indication that Plato had that in mind too, for the Stranger will presently say:

What we mean when we say "it appears" [is] a mixture of perception and belief (264 B1 f.).

He refers here to what we call perceptual judgments, and he will claim that these too must be true or false. "Theaetetus sits," whether vocalised or not, qualifies as such a mixture. It is a judgment about what appears, and perception comes into it. The two ingredients between them account for our perception of the sitting Theaetetus (the fact), and our belief that "Theaetetus sits." But the belief and therefore the statement can only be true in virtue of the fact, and only known to be true in virtue of our correct perception of the fact.

Plato does not *say* so. He will not by *word* accord sense-perception a key role to justify *hos estin* in proposition (a). He will not elevate the immediate perceptual awareness of simple facts to the status of *noësis*, which for him remains a mode of intellectual apprehension.[12] He lets the dramatic situation take over. The perceived fact enters the argument as a mute participant. We need not ask, how we know that the true statement is true. It is *shown* to be true. Whoever speaks the part of Theaetetus, sits.[13] And it is this person who is pointed to by the *peri sou* references.

The position is different, however, regarding the false statement. Although "Theaetetus flies" is palpably false, there cannot be any immediate, perceptual awareness of what is not the case. On the other hand, there is a logical criterion available to Plato, such as was lacking for the true statement. "Theaetetus flies" is false, because "Theaetetus sits" is true (and known to be true), and the two statements are incompatible. There is also, of course, an incompatibility between Theaetetus *qua* man and flying, i.e. between the subject and predicate of the false statement (which makes it necessarily false), but this is not at issue. For an incompatibility of this type does not serve as a criterion for contingently false statements nor for the Sophist's semblances. For these most likely would fail to deceive if there was no compatibility, no combination, at least in some respect, between subject and predicate. From this it would follow that we cannot unmask the Sophist, unless we know the truth about the matters on which he holds forth. There must be true statements, known to be true, with which his "spoken images" are incompatible. Again, we could not know that a contingently false statement, such as "Theaetetus is a shoemaker," was false, unless we knew the true statement with which it was incompatible.

To sum up, the truth of "Theaetetus sits" is a sufficient condition for "Theaetetus flies" to be false. But there is a two-way connection

---

[12] We may note Aristotle's struggle with the same problem and his wavering answers in *Eth. Nic.* 1142 A22 ff., 1143 B1–6, cp. 1147 A 25 ff.

[13] On the recitation (performance?) of Platonic dialogues see Gilbert Ryle (1966).

between true and false. As pointed out earlier, Plato was deeply concerned to prove the possibility of false statement, realizing perhaps that if all statements (logically) could not but be true, none could be true. We may therefore conclude that the falsity of "Theaetetus flies" (or any such incompatible statement) is a necessary (though not a sufficient) condition for "Theaetetus sits" to be true. It is not a sufficient condition, because ultimately truth must be intuitively perceived. But the possibility of falsehood provides a negative criterion in so far as a statement, to be true, must not be compatible with anything and everything.[14] That true statements are in these ways dependent on the possibility of false statements bears out our earlier hint (p. 96 f.) that there is an important sense in which true *logos*, too, has a share in not-being. It partakes of difference in relation to the infinite number of statements that are incompatible with it, and therefore false.

[14] Ackrill (1955) p. 205, makes this a criterion of meaning when he writes: "the statement 'Theaetetus is sitting' is a genuine informative statement only because it rules something out." I think, however, that Plato, in choosing his incompatible examples, was not so much concerned with meaning as with the conditions of true and false of any given statement, although the two issues can ultimately not be separated.

§ 24. The Being of false Logos

Plato has still to show, on the strength of his two examples, that false statements have being, that it is possible to say things that are-not, and yet say something (*legein ti*).

To anticipate, in order to maintain that it is possible to say things that are-not, Plato will break up the unity of the *logos* and surrender the incompatibility criterion of falsity which he has built into his examples. As a consequence he could still adhere to some form of correspondence, or even to Marten's identity as a criterion for true statements, but regarding false statements he would have to resort to incorrect combination, which by itself, as we found, is not sufficient. Moreover the move which is to enable him to say that false statements, *qua* saying things that are-not (*legein ta me onta*), are possible, will jeopardize the position that they are necessary as a condition of true statements *qua* true.

I will now recapitulate propositions (b)–(e), adding the Stranger's final definition of false statement (f):

(b) The false statement says things different from the things that are (*hetera ton onton*).

(c) Accordingly it says things that are-not (*legei ta me onta*) as things that are (*hos onta*).

(d) But things that are (*onta*), [though] different from things that are about you (*hetera onton peri sou*).

(e) For we said that about everything (*peri hekaston*) there are many things that are (*onta*) and also many that are-not (*ouk onta*).

(f) When what is said about you (*peri sou*), but so that what is different [*sc.* from what *is* about you] is said as the same [*sc.* as what *is* about you] or what is-not as what is (*me onta hos onta*), then it finally seems that, with such a combination (*synthesis*) of verbs and nouns formed, we get really and truly a false statement (263 D1–4).[1]

---

[1] [Bracketed amplifications following Hackforth (1945).]

We may note that the Stranger in his exposition does not start with the common view, that a false statement says things that are-not, which he accepts. He begins in (b) with his own analysis of false, which is based on the previously established sense of "is-not" as "is different from", and only then returns to the common view in (c). Moreover, in stating the common view, he adds the phrase "as things that are" (*hos onta*) so as to bring out its contradictory character. He implies that, given his analysis, the common view is acceptable, since the contradiction is only apparent: we can say the things that are-not as if they were, and "escape unscathed." His procedure here is reminiscent of his arguments exemplifying the interrelations of the very great kinds. There, too, his own analysis was recast in contradictory is/is-not terms (§ 17).[2]

On the face of it, (d) does no more than apply the analysis given in (b) to the special case of "Theaetetus flies" and the fact about him. The Greek text is compressed and requires an interpretative rendering. I have followed Cornford and taken *onta* to affirm the being of the things that are said: they *are*, even though they are other than the facts. This is what Plato wants to maintain, in order to beat the Sophist, and in proposition (e) he indicates why he thinks he can maintain it.

We have already discussed proposition (e), (p. 106). In giving his reason why the *hetera ton onton* have being, the Stranger merely recalls that there are many things that are and many that are-not in the case of everything. He thus generalises from, and applies to the case in hand, an earlier statement about forms. In the case of every form, the things that are or are-not are other forms in which it participates or in relation to which it participates in difference. In the case of Theaetetus they are represented by *praxeis*, the actions which he does or does-not perform, and which therefore are or are-not about him, i.e. in which he participates or in relation to which he participates in difference. The following moves, not spelled out in the text, are now available to the Stranger:

(i) Flying is a form. Forms partake of being. Flying is a thing that is.
(ii) Flying is a thing that is-not (in the case of Theaetetus). That which is-not is not something contrary to what is, but something that is different. Flying is a thing that is.

---

[2] E.g. "Motion participates in sameness and is different from sameness itself" was restated as "Motion is both the same and not the same," to which the Stranger added: "We must admit that and not be disturbed by it." The reason, of course, is that, on the strength of the preceding account, the contradiction is only apparent.

(iii) Flying is not-sitting. Not-sitting is part of the different. The different is. Not-sitting, being a part of the different, is. Flying is a thing that is.

(For (ii) and (iii) cp. § 19 on the Not-beautiful etc.) [3]

Leaving on one side for a moment the question whether the Sophist's position has been successfully controverted, we turn our attention to the rift that has occurred in passing from (d) to (e). Plato has switched from *onoma-rema* complex to *rema*, from statement to predicate, from fact to *praxis* (action). Perhaps he had no choice, for he could not prove – could he? – that "Theaetetus flying" has being.

Plato knew that "flying" and "sitting" are incompatible in virtue of their own nature, and he knew that "Theaetetus flies" and "Theaetetus sits" are incompatible statements. Plato may have reasoned, on the analogy of motion and rest, that although "sitting" and "flying" cannot participate in one another, both participate in being, and that the being of the one does not affect the being of the other. They are different "beings". We may put this by saying that when they are viewed in themselves *qua* forms, their incompatibility is not operative. Plato may have thought that the same holds of complex facts which they enter as determinations of things. And that is true enough in some cases. A bird flying and Theaetetus sitting are different facts. The being of the one does not affect the being of the other. The affirmations of those facts will each be either true or false, but the truth or falsity of the one has no bearing on the truth or falsity of the other. The incompatibility is still not operative. But it does become operative when it is a question of one and the same thing participating in both at the same time and in the same respect. The facts designated as "Theaetetus sitting" and "Theaetetus flying" affect one another in the sense that if the one *is* (the case), the other cannot *be*. The statements asserting these "facts" cannot both be true, and if the one is true, the other must be false. The being and not-being of what is asserted thus parallels the truth and falsity of the two statements. The incompatibility has become fully operative and cannot be relieved by an appeal to the predicates, for predicates are neither true nor false. As Plato knew, only statements are. In the case of incompatible statements, as distinct from incompatible predicates, being and not-being, like true and false,

---

[3] As pointed out earlier (p. 21 n. 2) Plato, though envisaging false denials, cannot deal with them. An application of (e) to the false statement "Theaetetus is not sitting" would involve him in the forms of "not-sitting" and of "not (not-sitting)" as part of the different. In (iii) this would engender the contradiction "Not-sitting" is "not (not-sitting)" or "Not-sitting is sitting."

are most opposed to one another. True and false *logoi*, and the being and not-being which they assert only partake of one another in the senses established earlier; without the possibility of saying what is false, and therefore is-not, we could not say what is true, and therefore is (the case), and without knowing true *logos* to be true, we could not know false *logos* to be false. Once the true/false incompatibility is diluted into difference, these important senses are lost: false *logos* ceases to be a necessary condition of true *logos* *qua* true, and our knowledge of a true statement can no longer be a sufficient condition for knowing that a false statement is false. But no other workable criterion is available. Plato has, unavoidably perhaps, shifted his ground, and it has not even helped him. "We must admit that, and not be disturbed by it."

We are not, however, entitled to read back the stance taken in (e) into the earlier *legein ta onta, legein ta me onta, hetera ton onton*. The *onta* etc. which a *logos* says are not what is referred to by its *rema* term, but what it asserts as a *plegma* (complex) of *onoma* and *rema*. See pp. 101 ff., 106 n. 8. It is not until (e) that the hard-won unity of *logoi* is sacrificed.

When we come to (f), the final definition, which occurs fourteen Stephanus lines below (e), it looks as though Plato felt the need to reaffirm the nature of *logos*, and this may account for bringing back the "combination (*synthesis*) formed from verbs and nouns," though here not spoken of as a *symploke* of verbs *with* nouns (262 D4). The phrase *me onta hos onta* is taken from (c), but "what is different as the same" (*thatera hos ta auta*) is new.[4] Since *thatera* is a *pros allo* term, it needs amplification, and this must be paired with a corresponding amplification of *ta auta*; I have adopted Hackforth's suggestions. *Thatera hos ta auta* is of course Plato's interpretation of *ta me onta hos onta*. We need to remember two things: (1) *Thatera* could only be proved as *onta* for the *rema* term, and this is bound to make the definition ambiguous; underneath the rift is still there. (ii) Difference is a formal character which only gives a necessary condition for false: what is false is different, but what is different from any given fact may also be the case. To make it a sufficient condition it needs sharpening into incompatibility, but this involves the material element, for things are

---

[4] It is by analogy with *thatera hos ta auta* that Marten (p. 108 n. 9) has coined the formula that the true statement "asserts the same as the same" (*ta auta hos ta auta*), and arrived at the idea that the true statement comprehends the "predicate" as identical with the action. The formula may be acceptable for the assertion of the fact as a complex whole.

incompatible, not in virtue of their participation in difference, but in virtue of their own natures.

In trying to refute the Sophist, Plato made, I believe, two mistakes. He thought he could avert *legein ta me onta = legein meden*, by showing that *legein ta me onta* in an important sense was still *legein ta onta*, and that, in turn, by showing that the predicate of the false statement was an *on*. He wanted the false statement to have reference, and thought that this would be provided by the signification of its predicate. But the reference of a false statement is provided by the reference of the incompatible true statement, while in a false statement we do assert what is-not (the case), irrespective of the "being signified" by the predicate, i.e. even though the predicate is an *on*. There is a sense of "is-not" which must be preserved for false statements, and Plato should have shown that it can be preserved without thereby falling into the Sophist's trap. But Plato only recognised two senses of "is-not," namely the Eleatic sense of "that which is in no way whatever" (§ 4) which is not a sense at all, and his own enlightened sense in which "is-not" can in all cases be rendered as "is different from". To escape from the former, Plato clung to the latter. It enabled him to retrieve the being of negative expressions, and there is a suspicion that he tried to vindicate false statements on the same lines, that he assimilated "Theaetetus flies," which is false, to the true negative statement "Theaetetus is not flying," treating "not-flying" as a single expression on the lines of the "not-beautiful." If this had been the correct procedure for vindicating the being of false statements, then it would indeed have been sufficient to show that flying is an *on*. "Theaetetus flies," when false, does of course imply "Theaetetus is not flying," but all that follows from this is the equivalence of the two expanded propositions, "Theaetetus flies is false" and "Theaetetus is not flying is true." But the statement "Theaetetus flies" is not asserted as false; it is asserted as true, it says *ta me onta hos onta* (propos. c.). Therefore, though false, it cannot be reduced to "Theaetetus is not flying" which is true, and the device will not work.

Since what is true is (the case), and what is false is incompatible with what is true, it cannot merely be different from what is true, but (unlike negative expressions) must be contrary to it, and hence there must be a genuine sense in which it is-not (the case). What is required is indeed not the total Parmenidean unstatable sense, but still an irreducible sense, that is to say, a weaker, contingent sense, which has no logically vitiating implications. This, however, was not available to

Plato, who was so preoccupied with the dismantling of the Parmenidean position that he had not left himself any opening for a straightforward denial of the existence of anything whatsoever (p. 76 above). And thus he could not fully exploit his deep insights into the nature of *logos* (p. 101) and the interdependence of true and false (p. 111 f.).

Bibliography

1. Text, Translations and Commentary

Platonis Opera, Tom. 1, recognovit J. Burnet (1900). Oxford, U.P.

Plato, *Sophist* with an Engl. transl. by H. N. Fowler (1921). London and Cambridge, Mass., the Loeb Classical Library.

Cornford, F. M. (1935), *Plato's Theory of Knowledge*, the *Theaetetus* and the *Sophist* of Plato translated with a running commentary. London, Kegan Paul.

2. Contemporary Literature referred to

Ackrill, J. L. (1955), "*Symploke Eidon*" in R. E. Allen, ed., *Studies in Plato's Metaphysics* (1965). London, Routledge and Kegan Paul.

Ackrill, J. L. (1957). "Plato and the Copula: *Sophist* 251–259" in R. E. Allen, ed., *Studies in Plato's Metaphysics* (1965). London, Routledge and Kegan Paul [originally published in *J. Hellenic Studies* LXXVII, pt. II (1957)].

Berger, F. R. (1965). "Rest and Motion in the *Sophist*," *Phronesis*, X, 1.

Bluck, R. S. (1957). "False Statement in the *Sophist*," *J. Hellenic Studies*, LXXVII, pt. II.

Broad, C. D. (1937). *The Mind and its Place in Nature*. London, Kegan Paul.

Cornford, F. M. (1937). *Plato's Cosmology*. London, Routledge and Kegan Paul.

Crombie, I. M. (1963). *An Examination of Plato's Doctrines*, vol. II. London, Routledge and Kegan Paul.

Frede, M. (1967). *Prädikation und Existenzaussage – Platons Gebrauch von "... ist ..." und "... ist nicht ..." im Sophistes* (Hypomnemata, 18). Göttingen, Vandenhoek & Ruprecht.

Gulley, N. (1962). *Plato's Theory of Knowledge*. London, Methuen.

Guthrie, W. K. C. (1965). *A History of Greek Philosophy*, Vol. II. Cambridge, U.P.

Guthrie, W. K. C. (1969). *A History of Greek Philosophy*, Vol. III. Cambridge, U.P.

Hackforth, R. (1945). "False Statement in Plato's *Sophist*," *Cl. Q.* XXXIX.

Hamlyn, D. W. (1955). "The Communion of Forms and the Development of Plato's Logic," *Phil. Q.*, 5, 21.

Kahn, C. H. (1966). "The Greek Verb 'to be' and the Concept of Being," *Foundations of Language* 2.

Kamlah, W. (1963). *Platons Selbstkritik im Sophistes* (Zetemata, 33). Munich, C. H. Beck.

Lorenz, K. and Mittelstrass, J. (1966). "Theaitetos fliegt – Zur Theorie wahrer und falscher Sätze bei Platon," *Arch. Gesch. Phil.*, 48, 2.

Malcolm, J. (1967). "Plato's Analysis of *to on* and *to me on* in the *Sophist*," *Phronesis*, XII, 2.

Marten, R. (1965). *Der Logos der Dialektik – Eine Theorie zu Platons Sophistes*. Berlin, de Gruyter.

Moravcsic, J. M. E. (1960). "*Symploke Eidon* and the Genesis of *Logos*," *Arch. Gesch. Phil.*, 42.

Moravcsic, J. M. E. (1962). "Being and Meaning in the *Sophist*," *Acta Philosophica Fennica*, XIV.

Mourelatos, P. D. (1970). *The Route of Parmenides*. New Haven and London, Yale U.P.

Owen, G. E. L. (1970). "Plato on Not-Being" in G. Vlastos ed., *Modern Studies in Philosophy: Plato I*. New York, Anchor Books.

Peck, A. L. (1952). "Plato and the *Megista Gene* of the *Sophist*: A Reinterpretation," *C.Q.* N.S. II.

Peck, A. L. (1962). "Plato's *Sophist*: The *Symploke ton Eidon*," *Phronesis*, VII, 1.

Prauss, G. (1966). *Platon und der logische Eleatismus*. Berlin, de Gruyter.

Ross, Sir David (1951). *Plato's Theory of Ideas*. Oxford, Clarendon Press.

Runciman, W. G. (1962). *Plato's Later Epistemology*. Cambridge, U.P.

Ryle, Gilbert (1965). "Dialectic in the Academy" in R. Bambrough ed., *New Essays on Plato and Aristotle*. New York, Humanities Press and London, Routledge and Kegan Paul.

Ryle, Gilbert (1966). *Plato's Progress*. Cambridge, U.P.

Sayre, K. M. (1969). *Plato's Analytic Method*. University of Chicago Press.

Stenzel, J. (1961). *Studien zur Entwicklung der Platonischen Dialektik von Sokrates zu Aristoteles*, 3. Auflage. Darmstadt, Wissenschaftliche Buchgesellschaft. Engl. ed.: *Plato's Method of Dialectic*, transl. and edited by D. J. Allan (1964). New York, Russell and Russell.

Taran, L. (1965). *Parmenides*. Princeton, New Jersey, U.P.

de Vogel, C. J. (1970). *Philosophia, Studies in Greek Philosophy*, Part I. Assen, van Gorcum & Comp.